Using
Photoshop 7

Robert Penfold

Bernard Babani (publishing) Ltd
The Grampians
Shepherds Bush Road
London W6 7NF
England
www.babanibooks.com

Please note

Although every care has been taken with the production of this book to ensure that any projects, designs, modifications, and/or programs, etc., contained herewith, operate in a correct and safe manner and also that any components specified are normally available in Great Britain, the Publisher and Author do not accept responsibility in any way for the failure (including fault in design) of any projects, design, modification, or program to work correctly or to cause damage to any equipment that it may be connected to or used in conjunction with, or in respect of any other damage or injury that may be caused, nor do the Publishers accept responsibility in any way for the failure to obtain specified components.

Notice is also given that if any equipment that is still under warranty is modified in any way or used or connected with home-built equipment then that warranty may be void.

© 2003 BERNARD BABANI (publishing) LTD

First Published - May 2003

British Library Cataloguing in Publication Data
A catalogue record for this book is available from the British Library

ISBN   0 85934 536 X

Cover Design by Gregor Arthur
Printed and bound in Great Britain by Cox and Wyman

Preface

Photoshop was introduced in 1987 and it rapidly became the standard program for image editing and manipulation. Now at version 7, Photoshop is a far more sophisticated and capable program that remains the standard choice processing images. I use a range of complex software, but I think it is probably fair to say that Photoshop 7 has more options and facilities than any of the others. This is not to say that it is exceptionally difficult to learn and use. The main reason for its success is the well thought out user interface that makes it reasonably straightforward to use. Anyone familiar with the basics of using computers and modern software should have no difficulty in using Photoshop to do some simple tasks.

On the other hand, learning to use Photoshop really proficiently takes time and effort, and some aspects of photo editing require skills that can only be obtained through experience. This book will not turn you into an instant Photoshop expert, but it does explain in simple terms how to use Photoshop to optimise image quality and how to exploit its creative potential. Be prepared to put in some time and effort experimenting with Photoshop, which is no great hardship and should be a lot of fun.

Photoshop is available in a Windows PC version and for Macintosh computers. The PC version was used in the production of this book, but in use there is very little difference between the two. The differences are mainly brought about by the use of different conventions in the way the two types of computer are used, and by differences in the nomenclature used in menus. Provided you are reasonably fluent in the use of a Macintosh computer you should have little difficulty following the methods described in this book. Even if you use the PC version you will still need to know the fundamentals of using the computer, but with either version you do not need to be a computer expert. No previous experience with graphics software is required to use this book.

This book can be used on its own to learn about Photoshop, but it is strongly recommended that it is used in conjunction with the program itself. The only way to learn about any creative software is to try it out, follow a few examples, and then try some ideas of your own. If you do not have a copy of Photoshop, PC and Macintosh demonstration programs can be downloaded from the Adobe web site (www.adobe.com), and these are fully operational for 30 days. About an hour or so per day for half that period should be sufficient to become reasonably skilled in using Photoshop. Using Photoshop with digital images will be quite a revelation if you are used to the restrictions of conventional film and professional processing. With digital imaging and Photoshop practically anything is possible.

Robert Penfold

Trademarks

Microsoft, Windows, Windows XP, Windows Me, Windows 98 and Windows 95 are either registered trademarks or trademarks of Microsoft Corporation. Photoshop and PageMaker are registered trademarks of Adobe Systems Inc.

All other brand and product names used in this book are recognised trademarks, or registered trademarks of their respective companies. There is no intent to use any trademarks generically and readers should investigate ownership of a trademark before using it for any purpose.

Contents

1

The basics 1

2

Ins and outs 45

3

Making selections 77

4

Selections and paths 115

5

Colour mixing 173

6

Colour balance 199

7

Brush tools 239

8

Filters and text............................ 291

1

The basics

Menus and palettes

Photoshop is a complex piece of software, but it is not difficult to learn the basics, such as loading a photograph, making changes to the contrast and colour balance, and saving the finished result. It can actually be used for applications other than processing digital images, such as "painting" your own digital image starting from a blank page. However, its primary application is photo editing, and book is largely concerned with using Photoshop in that role. Having learned the basics it is reasonably easy to move on to the more advanced facilities.

A normal Windows or Mac user interface relies on pop-down menus and toolbars, and the Photoshop is not too far removed from the norm. The problem with most graphics programs is that there are so many commands and parameters that can be adjusted; it becomes virtually impossible to accommodate everything using a totally standard user interface. Consequently, many graphics programs have the addition of floating toolboxes, palettes, or other gizmos that augment the usual menus and toolboxes.

Many programs have a customisable user interface, and Photoshop certainly falls into this category. Figure 1.1 shows the opening screen for my installation of Photoshop, but it will probably look slightly different if you install and run Photoshop on your computer. The top section of the window has the usual title and menu bars. Below these is a toolbar of sorts, but the main drawing and editing tools are accessed via the palette near the top left-hand corner of the window. This palette is a floating window, so it can be moved to any part of the main window using the standard dragging technique. Eventually you may prefer to relocate it, but initially it is probably best to leave it at or near its original position.

The right-hand section of the screen is used for various palettes, and it is really up to the user to choose what is and what is not displayed here. Like many modern programs, Photoshop's user interface is to some

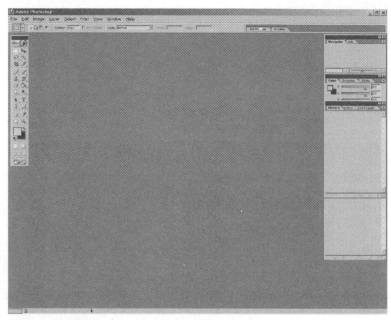

Fig.1.1 The normal screen layout of Photoshop

extent context sensitive, which simply means that it will change somewhat to suit the prevailing circumstances. The exact screen layout will therefore vary depending on how you set it up and what facilities you are using at the time, but the general scheme of things will remain like Figure 1.1. The menus and toolbar are at the top, the main tool palette is at the top left-hand corner, other palettes are on the right, and there is a large area for the image in the middle section of the screen. There is also the usual status bar along the bottom of the screen, and this shows some basic information such as the image's file size and the zoom ratio. It also provides a very brief explanation of how the currently selected tool is used.

Photoshop makes good use of the available screen area, but there is a definite advantage in using a high resolution screen. It is necessary to have a reasonably high resolution screen in order to display the images properly, but a significant amount of additional screen space is required for the palettes and the Toolbox. A minimum screen resolution of 1024 by 768 pixels is advisable, and a higher resolution of 1280 by 1024 pixels or more is definitely better. Incidentally, the screen shown in Figure 1.1

has a resolution of 1280 by 1024 pixels, as do all the screen dumps used in this book.

From scratch

As pointed out previously, Photoshop is primarily used for editing existing images, which are typically obtained from a scanner or a digital camera.

There is the option of producing a blank page and then drawing the image by hand. Photoshop is probably not the professional's first choice for this type of thing, but it has some quite powerful features if you wish to try your hand at digital painting and drawing. When initially experimenting with the program it is not a bad idea to produce a blank page and try some doodling. This

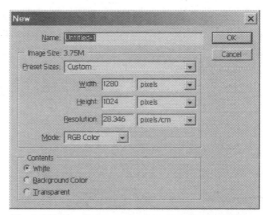

Fig.1.2 This dialogue box appears when New is selected from the File menu

is a good way to learn the basics of using brushes, which are as important for retouching photographs as they are for painting from scratch.

A blank page is produced by selecting New from the File menu, which produces the dialogue box of Figure 1.2. By default the new image will be called "Untitled1", but this can be changed to any valid filename by editing the contents of the relevant textbox. It is worth considering some of the other options in detail, as they are central to the operation of Photoshop.

Image size

By default this will probably be equal to the screen resolution in use. As already explained, this is 1280 by 1024 pixels in the case of my PC system, but it may well be different with your computer. Photoshop is primarily designed for bitmaps, where each image is made up from thousands or even millions of dots (pixels) of the appropriate colours. With the Custom option selected from the Preset Sizes menu it is possible to set any size within reason, but remember that the greater the number of pixels used, the larger the file size of the resultant image file.

Colour depth also has a large influence on file sizes. For instance, using 24-bit colour produces files three times larger than the same resolution used with 256 shades of grey. The image size is indicated near the top of the window, and the figure shown here will alter to suit changes in the resolution and colour depth.

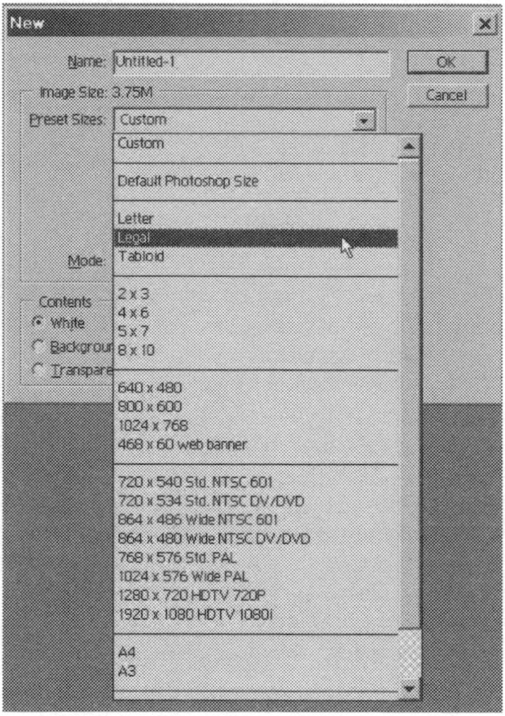

Memory is now much less of a problem than it was in the past. Equipping a computer with large amounts of memory is relatively inexpensive these days, and PCs with 512 megabytes of memory are now commonplace. It is still a factor that should not be ignored. A scan at 600 dots per inch should produce quite impressive looking results, but with 24-bit colour it produces over one megabyte of data per square inch, or about 100

Fig.1.3 Various preset sizes are available

megabytes of data from a full A4 scan. The usual recommendation for large files is that the amount of memory should be at least double the file size, so with the previous example some 128 megabytes of memory would be inadequate for good performance, but 256 megabytes would be more than adequate.

Resolution

There are several preset image sizes available from the pop-down menu (Figure 1.3), and one of these will often suffice. Some of these are paper sizes such as A4, rather than a size in the form X by Y pixels. When setting the width or height of a custom size, there is the option of using pixels, inches, centimetres, etc. (Figure 1.4). When the size of an image is set using pixels it is still possible to control the size of the image in millimetres (or whatever). Similarly, when setting the size in inches, centimetres, etc., it is still possible to control the number of pixels in the image.

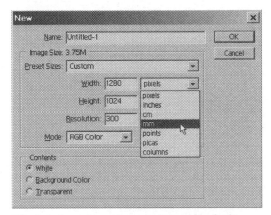

Fig.1.4 A custom size can be set in pixels, inches, centimetres, etc.

The relationship between the physical image size and the number of pixels is controlled by the figure used in the Resolution textbox. With the resolution at (say) 1200 by 900 pixels and the resolution at 300 pixels per inch, the image would be 4 inches by 3 inches. If this was too small the image could be made larger by reducing the resolution to 200 pixels per inch, which would increase the size to 6 by 4.5 inches. When setting the physical size of the image, the number of pixels can be raised by increasing the resolution, or decreased by reducing it.

In theory at any rate, by juggling with the resolution figure it is possible to set any page size and then set any desired number of pixels. Alternatively, the size in pixels can be set first, with the physical size of the image then being controlled by the resolution setting. On the face of it, there is no need to bother too much about the physical size of an image until it is printed out or exported to another program such as a DTP (desktop publishing) type. The size can be altered when the image is printed, and DTP programs enable the size of a loaded image to be altered.

Size matters

In practice it is usually best if the image size is set early in the proceedings. Suppose an image having 1200 by 900 pixels and a physical size of 4 by 3 inches is loaded into a DTP program, and that the image is then resized to 12 by 9 inches. This will work in the sense that the image will have the desired size, but trebling its size on both dimensions reduces an initial resolution of 300 pixels per inch to just 100 pixels per inch. Setting the resolution too low results in the pixels being clearly visible, and produces some very rough looking results.

Reducing the size to 2 by 1.5 inches would have the opposite effect, with the resolution being boosted to 600 pixels per inch. This gives the potential for higher output quality, but an excessively high resolution can also give problems with some printing processes. Setting a resolution that is beyond the capabilities of the output device will not give increased quality. In addition to potential problems with some printing processes, it can be counterproductive due to the file sizes involved. Excessive resolution produces larger file sizes, which can give problems when exporting images to programs such as word processors and DTP programs. It can be particularly troublesome where numerous images are involved, and the total file size can be quite large anyway.

There is no "hard and fast" figure at which resolution becomes inadequate. It depends on factors such as the type of image and the printing process used. In general, most people are reasonably happy with photographic images having a resolution of 200 pixels per inch, but notice graininess or even the individual pixels at a resolution as low as 150 pixels per inch. The minimum acceptable resolution for most people is therefore somewhere between these two figures. Note that you have to be careful with the resolution of an image whether it is built up from scratch, scanned, or loaded from a digital camera. Whatever the source, the same rules apply. If the resolution is too low the individual pixels will be visible.

Monitor resolution

The default resolution is usually 72 dots per inch, or just over 28 dots per centimetre. This is clearly rather low and inadequate for most purposes. This resolution is used by default as it is the typical resolution of a monitor, but the exact resolution obviously varies from one monitor to another, and also depends on the mode in use. In general, relatively low resolution is acceptable for applications such as web pages, where the final output will be displayed on a monitor rather than printed out. If the final output will be via a monitor it is not really necessary to bother too much about the resolution figure. Just set an appropriate image size in pixels.

Do not fall into the trap of thinking that an image will print out properly at (say) 200 by 150 millimetres because it looks all right at that size on the monitor. The size normally has to be reduced substantially in order to obtain adequate print quality. This is demonstrated by the fact that a monitor has a typical resolution of 72 dots per inch, while an absolute minimum of nearly 200 dots per inch is required for prints. Inkjet printers often have resolutions of 1200 dots per inch or even higher. In most cases this is very misleading, because the colours are mixed on the paper using several printer dots per image pixel. The true resolution is therefore much lower than the simple dots per inch figure for the printer. It will still be much higher than for a monitor though.

Mode and Contents

Colour modes is a subject that will be covered in a later chapter. For initial experiments the default RGB (red, green, blue) setting will suffice. This is the colour system used by monitors, which mix the three primary colours to make all the other colours.

The Contents menu has three radio buttons that permit the initial contents of the new page to be set. The White option simply gives a white background, and the Background option uses whatever background colour is set at the time. The Transparent option is analogous to drawing on a sheet of transparent film. Anything on layers behind the current one will show through the blank areas on the current layer. Layers are another topic that is covered in detail in a later chapter.

Resizing

With any image, whether produced from scratch or loaded from a scanner, etc., it is possible to increase or reduce its size. There are two distinctly different types of resizing though. With one it is the page size that is being altered and not the image. In other words, anything already on the page remains unaltered if the page is made larger, with additional blank space being added around the existing image. Reducing the page size has the opposite effect, with the outer area of the existing image being cut off. This is usually termed clipping or cropping.

Pixels are added or removed if the image size is altered, but it is done in such a way that the image looks much the same. This may seem pointless, but it is actually a very useful facility. Suppose that you have a high resolution scanned image that you wish to use for a web page. The layout of the web page might require an image having about 300 by 200 pixels, but the original image could have a resolution of 3000 by 2000 pixels or more. Getting Photoshop to resize the image to 300 by 200 pixels will produce a suitable image for the web page.

Image quality

There are a couple of important points to bear in mind when reducing the number of pixels in an image. The first and more obvious one is that the reduction in the number of pixels produces a reduction in the quality of the image. Whether this is of any practical importance depends on the nature of the image. In general, it is best to keep the subject very simple if the final resolution will be very low.

For example, a close-up of a face should be quite recognisable if it is reduced to a low resolution image, but the same is unlikely to be true of a photograph showing a full-length view of 20 or 30 people. The group shot might still serve its purpose in low resolution form, but there is a risk that it will look like nothing much at all. It is unlikely that anyone in the image will be recognisable if each head is produced by a few pixels. The only way to find out if a low resolution image is adequate for your intended purpose is to try it and then make a subjective judgement. The chances of success will always be much better with simple subject matter.

The second point to bear in mind is that having reduced the size of an image, taking it back up to the original size will not restore the original image. Information is lost when the image is reduced in size. Photoshop can be used to add pixels and take the image back up to the original number of pixels, but it can not put back the missing detail. This point is demonstrated by Figures 1.5 and 1.6. Figure 1.5 is the original image, which 400 by 300 pixels. Figure 1.6 is the result of reducing the image to 100 by 75 pixels and then restoring it to the original size. The loss of definition is very pronounced.

Consequently, it is important to use a copy of an image when the number of pixels in the image will be reduced. If you need a high resolution version of the image it is then just a matter of returning to the original image file. In fact it is a good idea to always work on a copy of an image when working with something like a picture from a digital camera, where there is no way of obtaining the image again if the original is ruined. It is less important to work on a copy with something like a scanned photograph. If the worst came to the worst it would presumably take no more than a minute or two to rescan the photograph. Many digital camera users archive all images in their original state on some form of read-only media such as CD-R discs. The archive images can not be accidentally altered or overwritten, so you always have the option of going back to the original image if this should be necessary for some reason.

Fig.1.5 The original image

Fig.1.6 The reduced and restored version

More pixels

Photoshop can be used to artificially boost the number of pixels in an image, but again, adding pixels will not add detail to the image. It can still be useful to boost the number of pixels in an image, but you need to be aware of the limitations of doing this. The usual reason for increasing the number of pixels is that you have a low resolution image, perhaps from a low resolution digital camera or downloaded from a web page. You would like to do a printout of the image, but at 200 dots per inch it is reproduced at little more than the size of a large postage stamp. Reducing the resolution to 75 or 100 dots per inch gives a more reasonable print size, but the pixels are large and obvious.

Fig.1.7 Stepping is very obvious on some parts of this zoomed view

Keeping the resolution at 200 dots per inch but doubling or trebling the number of pixels in each axis should give much more convincing results. The image area is increased by a factor of four and nine respectively, but the pixel size remains the same. Although no detail has been added to the image, the pixels are kept small and unnoticeable. Simply scaling up an image tends to produce noticeable stepping on diagonal lines, but this is absent when the pixel count is increased as well.

Figure 1.7 shows a highly zoomed view of a photograph, and stepping is very noticeable in a number of places. It is particularly noticeable in parts of the line around the nameplate. Figure 1.8 shows the result of increasing the vertical resolution from 300 to 1500 pixels, with the horizontal resolution also being subjected to a fivefold increase. There is clearly no more detail in the boosted version, and if anything it looks a fraction "softer" than the original version.

Where necessary, further processing can be used to sharpen an image that suffers from this problem. Although the sharpness may sometimes look fractionally worse, the stepping in the line around the nameplate

Fig.1.8 Increasing the number of pixels has smoothed the stepping

and the lettering is much less apparent in the version that has more pixels. Stepping gives very rough looking results and it is important to avoid it if at all possible.

Unpredictable results

It is only fair to point out that odd things can happen when an image is scaled up or down. There should be no major problems if the mathematics are simple, and the image has the number of pixels in each dimension doubled, trebled, halved, or whatever. In rare cases things can still go slightly awry though.

Suppose there is a vertical line in an image that is one pixel wide. With the number of pixels halved in each dimension, leaving the line in the image effectively doubles its width. Simply removing it might result in an important element of the image being omitted. Including some pixels and omitting others would be unlikely to give convincing results either.

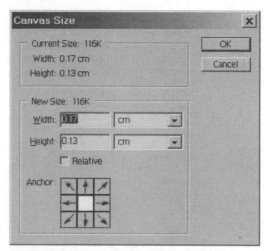

Fig.1.9 The Canvas Size dialogue box

Large reductions in the number of pixels will inevitably require some compromises in the fine detail.

If the number of pixels is boosted by an odd amount such as 1.57 times in each dimension, the mathematics are not straightforward and compromises have to be made. Photoshop is very good at avoiding obvious problems, and it is good at maintaining detail when the number of pixels is reduced. However, there is no guarantee that the processed image will be entirely glitch free. Low resolution images are more prone to scaling problems than the high resolution variety.

Increased page size

The page size can be increased by selecting Canvas Size from the Image menu. This produces a window like the one in Figure 1.9, where new X and Y dimensions can be set. The default sizes are in centimetres, but the pop-down menus give other options such as inches, percent, and pixels. The "map" controls where the additional space will be placed, or the part of the image that will be cropped if the page size is reduced. In the example of Figure 1.10 the white square representing the original page has been placed in the middle square of the bottom row. Accordingly, the additional page space has been added above and to the sides of the image.

It is not necessary to change both the width and height dimensions. Suppose that additional space is required above the image but not to the sides. The white square representing the original image would again be placed in the middle of the bottom row, and the height setting would be increased. The width setting would be left unaltered though, so that no additional space was added at the sides of the image. A similar system can be used to crop one or two sides of the image. In Figure 1.11 the white square has been placed in the centre of the "map", and the height setting has been reduced slightly. This has cropped the top and bottom of the photograph but has

Fig.1.10 *The canvas has been enlarged above and on both sides of the image*

left the sides unchanged. Note though, that there are other ways of cropping images, and in most cases the alternatives are better.

Changing image size

The image size is changed by selecting Image Size from the Image menu, and this produces the control panel of Figure 1.12. Keep the Constrain Proportions checkbox ticked if you wish ensure that the original aspect ratio of the image can not be altered. In DTP it can often be useful to stretch an image in order to fit it into the available space, but it is advisable to keep this type of thing to a minimum. Even quite small changes in the

aspect ratio can be very obvious with some images. It tends to be very noticeable when pictures of people or familiar animals such as horses are stretched or compressed.

If the Resample Image checkbox is not ticked, the number of pixels in

Fig.1.11 *Here the height of the canvas has been reduced, cropping the top and bottom of the image*

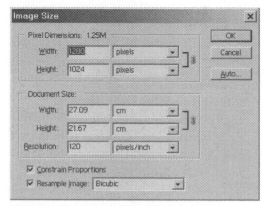

Fig.1.12 The Image Size dialogue box

the image will be locked and only the physical size and resolution can then be altered. With this checkbox ticked it is possible to alter the number of pixels, and Photoshop will automatically recalculate and display the new version of the image when the OK button is operated. Changes to the physical size and resolution settings will result in the number of pixels being changed, and the new size of the image in pixels will be shown in the upper section of the window.

A change in the number of pixels will change the physical size of the image. For example, a doubling of the number of pixels in each dimension will also double the physical size of the image in each direction. Often what is required is an increase or decrease in the pixel count with no attendant change in the physical size. An easy way around the problem is to use the Image Size command twice. Use it the first time with the Resample Image function enabled, so that the pixel count can be altered. Then use the command again with the Resample Image function disabled, so that the size can be altered without altering the pixel count. The original size can be restored or a new size can be set.

Toolbox

While the Photoshop menu system is undoubtedly an important part of the program that you will need to use a great deal, the Toolbox contains the facilities that are used the most when creating images or editing photographs. Figure 1.13 shows the Toolbox and gives a brief description of each tool. Photoshop has evolved over the years, with more and more tools being added. Some of the buttons have more than one function in order to keep the Toolbox reasonable small. The multifunction buttons are the ones that have a small triangle in the bottom right-hand corner. Right-clicking on one of these buttons produces a small popup menu (Figure 1.14), and the desired function for the button is then selected

Adobe Online		
Marquee Tools		Move Tool
Lasso Tools		Magic Wand
Crop Tool		Slice Tools
Healing/Patch Tool		Paintbrush/Pencil
Rubber Stamp		History Brush
Eraser Tools		Gradient/Paint Bucket
Blur/Sharpen/Smudge		Dodge/Burn/Saturate
Path Selection Tools		Text Tools
Path Tools		Shape/Line Tools
Notes Tools		Colour Tools
Hand Tool		Zoom Tool
Foreground Colour		Switch Colours
Default Colours		Background Colour
Standard Mode		Quick Mask Mode
		Screen Modes
Image Ready		

Fig.1.13 Details of Photoshop's Toolbox. Note that many of the buttons have more than one function

in the usual way. It may take a while to get used to the icons on the buttons, but positioning the pointer over a button produces a small popup message showing the name of the tool it selects. These little popup messages appear when the pointer is placed over any pointer, plus some tabs, etc.

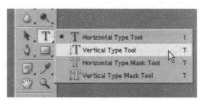

Fig.1.14 One of the popup menus

Selection tools

The large button at the top can be used to look for program updates via the Internet, and it can also be used to set up regular background searches for updates. Most of the other buttons are arranged with buttons having similar functions grouped together. The group nearest the top are the selection tools, which are used to select all or part of an image so that it can be processed in some way. In general, these tools do not provide any processing themselves, with the exceptions of the Move and Crop tools. With these you can move or crop (trim) the selection, which is a quick way of handling things provided a fairly basic selection process will suffice. The Slice tool is mainly for use with web page design, and it enables the page to be divided into areas that are saved as separate files.

The other three tools are the main selection tools. The Magic Wand tool is intended as a quick way of making a complex selection. You simply click at a suitable point on the image and it then marks out an area or several areas based on the colours or shades in the image. It looks for adjacent pixels of the same or similar shade or colour. It is a system that works well if the required area has a dark outline against a

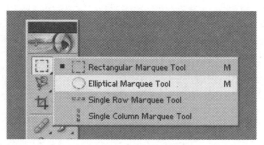

Fig.1.15 Four versions of the Marquee tool are available

black background or something equally convenient. Of course, in practice this will not always be the case, and an alternative selection method then has to be used.

Using the Marquee tool it is possible to drag a shape onto the screen, and this marks the selected area. A rectangle is used by default, but three other options are available (Figure 1.15). The name of the tool is derived from the fact that the outline of the selection is indicated by small lines of flashing pixels, which are like the flashing lights on a circus marquee. The point of the flashing pixels is to make outline of the selection clearly standout against any background. The default Lasso tool permits an area to be

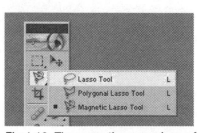

Fig.1.16 There are three versions of the Lasso tool

selected by drawing a freehand shape onto the screen. A couple of variations are available, as shown in Figure 1.16. One of these enables a shape to be built up from a series of straight lines. The second gives a sort of cross between the freehand and Magic Wand methods. Note that it is possible to use a combination of selection methods to produce complex selections.

Painting tools

As one would probably expect, the Painting tools are used to paint or draw onto the "canvas". These tools imitate real drawing and painting implements, such as a paintbrush and a pencil. The Clone Stamp tool enables an area of the image to be copied to another area. This is mainly used when retouching a photograph. You paint over a blemish in the image using material copied from a part of the image that has a suitable texture and colour. If you use Photoshop with a digital camera or a scanner you will probably use the Clone Stamp tool a great deal. Incidentally, it is known simply as the Clone tool to most users and this is the name that will be used in this book.

The Airbrush tool had its own button in the Toolbox in versions as far as Photoshop 6, but this has been dropped in Photoshop 7. Instead, it is available as an option on the Brushes palette. This palette can be launched by selecting Brushes from the Window menu, or by operating the Brushes tab on the Options bar. Either way, the Brushes palette will appear in the top right-hand corner of the screen (Figure 1.17). There are several checkboxes down the left-hand side of the palette, and one of these (the third from bottom) is used to enable or disable the airbrush facility. The airbrush facility can also be toggled on and off via its button on the Options bar.

Any size or shape of brush can be used as an air type, even when using a tool such as the Clone tool. The difference between an airbrush and a standard type is that an airbrush can be used to gradually build up paint. This is possible using an ordinary brush by repeatedly brushing an area, but it can be achieved with an airbrush even if it is kept still. This often makes it easier to obtain the desired effect if less than complete coverage is required.

Erasers

There are several erasers to choose from. The standard version operates much like the Paintbrush tool, but it paints the background colour onto the screen. The Background version of the Eraser tool is the one I tend

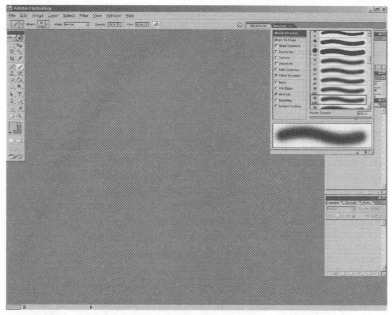

Fig.1.17 The Brushes palette has dropped down from the Options bar

Fig.1.18 The Background Eraser tool removes everything on a layer, including the background

to think of as the "proper" eraser, and it totally removes the affected part of a layer, not even leaving the background colour. Any layer or layers behind the current one will show through the gaps left in the image by this eraser.

If there are no layers behind the current one, a check pattern will show through at the points where the image is erased

(Figure 1.18). This check pattern is Photoshop's way of telling you that there is a hole in the image, where there is not even a background colour. Note that this pattern is not used when an image is printed, saved, exported, etc. The empty areas of the image are coloured white, and the check pattern is merely used as a means of keeping the user informed about what the program is doing.

The third version of the Eraser tool is the Magic Eraser. This has similarities to the Magic Wand tool, and it is what I suppose could be considered a colour-conscious tool. If you click on a pixel using this tool, it erases that pixel and any adjacent ones of the same colour. It will then erase any pixels of the same colour that are adjacent to those pixels, and so on, moving outward until no further pixels of the right colour can be found. The tolerance setting on the Options bar enables this tool to be very fussy about pixels being the right colour, to be very easy going, or anywhere in between.

New tools

Photoshop 7 has several new Painting tools, and one of these is the Healing Brush. This is similar to the Clone tool, and it is mainly used for retouching blemishes in photographic images. It is a sort of "intelligent" version of the Rubber Stamp tool that tries to limit the copying to the damaged part of the print, filling in the blemish as seamlessly as possible. The cloned material has its colour and luminosity matched to the surrounding area. The Patch version of the Healing tool provides the same basic area, but you select the damaged area and then an area on the image that will be used to patch the faulty area.

The History Brush is used in conjunction with the History palette. The latter shows a list of the recent commands and it enables the user to step back through these stages to undo mistakes. There is also a standard Undo/Redo facility available from the Edit menu, together with a multi-level Step Forward and Step Backward function. The History palette provides a quicker and easier means of moving backwards and forwards through large numbers of steps. The History Brush enables parts of the image to be painted with an earlier version of the image. For example, you could add a filter effect and then selectively remove it from parts of the image. The Art History Brush is similar and is mainly used for special effects.

The Gradient tool is a variation on the Paint Bucket tool. The Paint Bucket tool simply fills a selected area with the current foreground colour, or a flood-fill as this is sometimes called. The Gradient tool also provides a form of flood-fill, but the fill is not all the same colour. Instead, start and finished colours are specified, and the fill changes from one to the other. There are plenty of variations that enable the angle of the fill to be controlled, provide radial rather than linear fills, and so on.

Sharpen, Blur, etc.

The Sharpen and Blur tools do more or less what their names suggest. The Sharpen tool "hardens" "soft" edges and tends to produce a localised boost in contrast. The Blur tool does the opposite of this. There is also a Smudge option available from this button. When using this tool it is like smearing wet paint using your finger, and it is mainly for producing special effects. However, it can also be used to reduce unwanted texture in an area of the image.

Equivalents to photographic printing techniques are available from the Dodge and Burn tools. Dodging and burning are simple techniques for increasing or decreasing the exposure in certain parts of a photographic print. The Dodge and Burn tools provide digital versions of these functions, and they respectively lighten and darken the affected parts of the image. There is a Sponge tool available from the same button. Depending on the setting in the Options bar, this tool will saturate or desaturate the processed section of the image. In other words, it makes the colours stronger or weaker.

Text, etc.

The next group of buttons provide a range of functions that involve adding material to an image, but they are not really what could be described as painting tools. As one would expect, the Text tool enables text to be added to an image. Horizontal and vertical text options are available, in addition to mask versions of these. The mask versions produce a mask that follows the outline of the lettering, and the Brush tool, etc., can then be used to fill the mask with the required colour scheme.

Rectangles filled with the current background colour can be produced using the Rectangle tool, but there are several options for this button (Figure 1.19). These enable shapes such as ellipses, polygons, and rectangles with rounded corners to be produced. There is also a Custom Shape option that permits a library of your own shapes to be produced. A number of custom shapes are included in the default set (Figure 1.20), and these are useful even if you are not inclined to produce your own.

Photoshop is primarily concerned with bitmaps, but it also has some vector graphics capability. With vector graphics the image is not stored as a set of pixels. Instead, it is stored as a database detailing the positions and other characteristics of lines and shapes. The lines and shapes can be complex curves and intricate shapes, and not just simple straight lines, circles, etc.

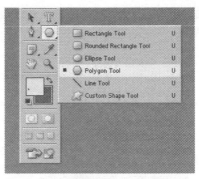

Fig.1.19 Several alternative shapes are available

An advantage of vector graphics is that the system is largely resolution independent. What this means in practice is that zooming in on an image or printing it large does not produce huge pixels. Diagonal lines and curves remain free from stepping provided the resolution of the output device is up to the task. Vector graphics are good for things like charts, diagrams, and technical drawings, but this method is not of much use for storing photographic images. Photographic images are too complex and do not conveniently break down into a few dozen lines and shapes with simple fills. Another advantage of vector graphics is that the lines and shapes are easily edited via control points. If a shape is not quite right, simply drag the control points to produce precisely the required shape.

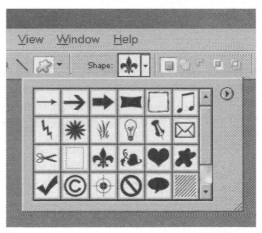

Fig.1.20 The default set of custom shapes

Photoshop tries to provide the best of both worlds by combining bitmaps with vector graphics. A photographic image can be loaded and then vector graphic shapes and lines can be added. Note that resolution independence will be lost if the image is saved or exported in a bitmap format such as the popular Jpeg format. Keep copies of images in Photoshop's native PSD format if you wish to retain the ability to edit any vector graphics within the images.

In addition to the shapes available from the various Shape tool options, it is possible to draw lines and shapes using the Pen tool. Complex curves and shapes can be produced using this tool. Lines drawn rather than painted onto the screen are called paths in Photoshop terminology. Hence the Path Selection tools are used when selecting and editing drawn lines and shapes. Straight lines can be drawn using the Line tool, and the lines can be constrained to angles of 0 degrees, 45 degrees, 90 degrees, etc., by holding down the Shift key while dragging them onto the screen.

Zoom, etc.

The next group of four tools provide some relatively simple but very important facilities. The Zoom tool enables a small part of the image to be expanded to fit the drawing window. This is more than a little helpful when "fine tuning" images. This tool works in standard fashion, with a box being dragged onto the screen to define the area that will be included in the zoomed view. That part of the image will then be made as large as possible without any of it being lost off the edge of the image window. It is also possible to zoom in at a ratio of about 1.5 to 1 by left-clicking at the centre of the area you wish to enlarge. It is possible to zoom out in the same way, but with the Alt key (Option key on Macs) held down while the mouse is clicked.

The image becomes too big to fit on the screen when a zoomed view is used, but the usual scrollbars can be used to pan around the picture so that any desired part of it can be viewed without having to zoom out and in again. An alternative method of panning around a zoomed picture is to use the Hand tool. In effect, this tool grabs the image and pulls it across the window. You can therefore drag the image around the screen until the required section is displayed.

This tool works in real-time, with the picture being continuously redrawn to take into account changes in position. As a result, it is very easy to pan to precisely the required area of the image. Early attempts at real-time panning often produced very jumpy results with a lot of screen-flicker. Provided a reasonably powerful PC and a good graphics card are used, the Photoshop panning systems all give smooth and flicker-

Fig.1.21 The main view can be panned via the Navigation palette

free results. Here is a useful ploy to remember. The Hand tool can be produced in place of the current tool simply by holding down the Space Bar. Simply release the Space Bar in order to return to the current tool.

The Navigation panel is usually displayed near the top right-hand corner of the screen (Figure 1.21), and this shows a miniature ("thumbnail") version of the image. A red rectangle on this indicates the area of the picture currently displayed in the main window. An alternative method of panning is to use the Hand tool to drag the rectangle around the thumbnail view. Again, this pans the main view in real-time, so you can look at the main view to "fine tune" the position of the rectangle.

The Notes tool can be used to add notes to yourself or others working on the image, rather like the sticky yellow notes that many people use to decorate their refrigerator. Having added a note, right-click on it and use the popup menu to open, close, or delete it. The notes are only displayed on the screen, and will not be included on any images that are printed or exported. Apparently it is possible to record and playback audio notes with a suitably equipped computer, but I have never tried this facility.

Colour selection

The fourth button in this group is for the Eyedropper tool. This is used to set the current foreground colour by left-clicking with it at a suitable point on the screen. In other words, an existing colour in the image can be selected and you can then paint with that colour. Note that the Photoshop version of the Eyedropper tool only works within the image window. It is not possible to select a colour from elsewhere on the screen. Of course, the windows and palettes that provide colour swatches and colour mixing facilities are an exception.

When using the Eyedropper tool in a finely textured area of a picture it can be awkward to pick out the required colour. Zooming in on the relevant area of the image makes the task very much easier. In the section of the Toolbox below Eyedropper tool there are two overlapping squares that show the current foreground and background colours. The

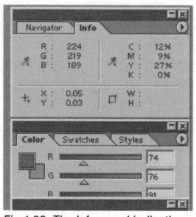

Fig.1.22   The Info panel indicating colour values

foreground square will change to the selected colour, and it will therefore be obvious if the wrong colour has been selected. The required colour can usually be picked out without too much difficulty, but it might take two or three attempts.

The Color Sampler is offered as an alternative to the Eyedropper tool. This can be used to place up to four markers on the image area, and the Information panel will show the colour values of the currently selected marker. The Info panel is normally grouped with the Navigation palette, and it will automatically appear on top when the Color Sampler tool is in use. To remove a marker, simply drag it out of the image window. When active, the Info panel will show colour information for the pixel that the Eyedropper tool is currently over (Figure 1.22). An advantage of the marker system is that you do not have to keep the pointer still while trying to read the colour information. You can carefully manoeuvre the marker into position and it will not budge unless you move it.

There is a third option in the form of the Measuring tool. This can be used to drag a line onto the screen, and the Options bar then indicates the co-ordinates for the end points, plus the length and angle of the line. It can therefore be used to provide dimension information about existing objects in the image. The end points and the line itself can be dragged so that the line can be easily manoeuvred into exactly the required position. The line automatically disappears when a different tool is selected, and it will not be printed, exported, or saved with the rest of the image.

Colour swap

As pointed out previously, the next section of the Toolbox has two overlapping squares that show the current background and foreground colours. These are used as the default colours for painting, drawing, and fill operations, but in Photoshop terminology they are the current colours rather than the default colours. The default background and foreground colours are white and black respectively. These can be selected using the small button just to the left of the background square in the Toolbox.

The small button in the top right-hand corner can be used to swap the foreground and background colours. One use of this facility is to permit the background colour to be set using the Eyedropper tool. Swap the foreground and background colours, select the required background colour using the Eyedropper tool, and then swap the foreground and background colours again. This gives the desired result with the background set to the selected colour and the foreground colour left unchanged.

Options bar

The Options bar was the Options palette up to Photoshop 5, but in versions 6 and 7 it is the toolbar just beneath the menu bar. It is the convention to have a toolbar beneath the menu bar, but the buttons on

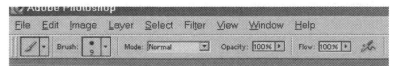

Fig.1.23 The Options bar is immediately below the menu bar

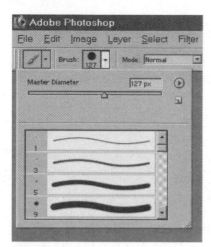

Fig.1.24 The pop-down Brush

the toolbar normally offer commonly used facilities such as Save, Copy, Paste, etc. In Photoshop these facilities can only be accessed via the menu system or keyboard shortcuts, and they are not available from the Options bar.

The Options bar is an important part of Photoshop, and one of its functions is to supply information to the user. It can also be used to "fine tune" various functions so that they operate exactly as required. The Options bar is context sensitive, so its precise function alters to suit the tool in use at the time. Try selecting

Fig.1.25 The Options bar is context sensitive. This is the version for the Gradient tool

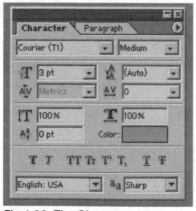

Fig.1.26 The Character palette

different tools from the Toolbox and you will find that there are nearly as many versions of the Options bar as there are tools. Some very similar tools such as the brush types do utilize what is essentially the same version of the Options bar.

Figure 1.23 shows the bar with the Brush tool selected. This enables the opacity to be controlled, a different mode to be selected, and the Airbrush function to be enabled. There is also a pop-down menu that offers various preset brush sizes and types (Figure 1.24), and a slider control to permit adjustment of the brush diameter. Figure 1.25 shows the Options bar with the Gradient tool selected, and most of the options have changed. The Opacity control remains, but there are now buttons to select the type of gradient fill required, a menu offering various preset fill types, and so on. The appropriate options are offered for whatever tool is selected at the time.

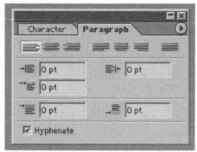

Fig.1.27 The Paragraph palette controls text alignment, hyphenation, etc.

Palette button

There is a button set away from the others on the Option bar, well towards the right end of the bar. Where appropriate, this activates the palette or palettes that are relevant to the selected tool. For example, with the Text tool selected, operating this button produces the Character and Paragraph palettes (Figure 1.26). The Character palette is displayed by default, but operating the appropriate tab switches to the Paragraph palette (Figure 1.27). With the Brush tool selected, the Brush palette is displayed when this button is operated (Figure 1.28). This button

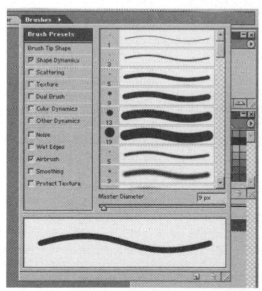

Fig.1.28 The Brush palette provides a number of options

*Fig.1.29 The Options bar can be docked near the bottom of the
screen (as here) or used as a floating bar*

does not appear on the Options bar if there is no palette that matches
the selected tool. For example, it is not included when the Marquee tool
is selected.

Like any of the Windows, the Options bar can be switched on an off via
the Windows menu. Since it is so central to the operation of Photoshop
it is not advisable to switch it off for long. Once switched off it can be
reactivated again via the Windows menu or by double-clicking on any
tool icon in the Toolbox. The Options bar can be dragged to a different
position by latching the pointer onto the extreme left end of the bar. It
can either be used as a floating bar or docked at the bottom of the screen,
as in Figure 1.29.

Note that anything on the Options bar that has a small triangle beside it
has some sort of popup available by right-clicking on the triangle. In the
example of Figure 1.30 a menu has been produced, but there are other
popup items such as slider controls.

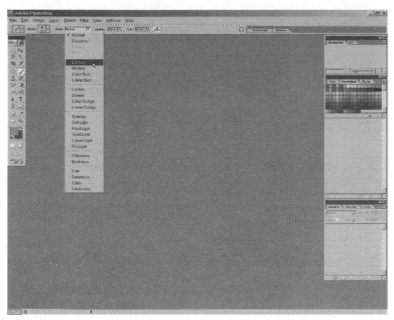

Fig.1.30 The options bar usually has one or two pop-down menus

Menus

Some of the menus are the sort of thing that can be found in practically any modern software. The File menu is used when opening or saving files, importing and exporting images, and so on. The standard file browser is available (Figure 1.31), and this shows a thumbnail of the selected image file. An alternative file browser is available from the Windows menu or the tab on the Options bar (Figure 1.32). This "new" feature shows a thumbnail picture for each file, making selection easier if you are not sure of the correct filename for the required image. I had a graphics program 20 years ago that had this feature, so it is perhaps surprising that it has only appeared quite recently in Photoshop and several other graphics programs.

The Windows menu is also fairly standard, and it is used to open or close any of the Windows, most of which are palettes or panels, depending on your preferred terminology. The Edit menu also has several familiar functions such as Cut, Copy, and Paste, together with some more

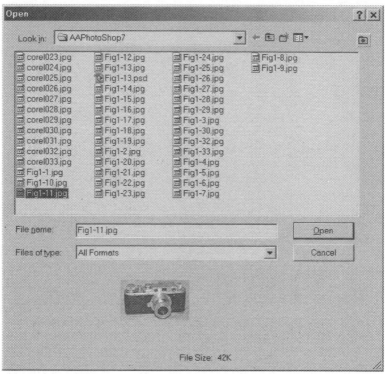

Fig.1.31 The standard version of the file browser is available

advanced functions such as a spelling checker and a Find and Replace Text function.

Most graphics programs have the ability to spread the image over several layers. This is analogous to drawing or painting a picture onto pieces of transparent film placed one on top of the other. Some areas of the lower layers are visible while others are blocked by higher layers. Using layers makes it easy to alter some parts of the image while leaving others unchanged, and it is a system that is much used in animation. Photoshop can use numerous layers and has a comprehensive range of controls for handling them. These have their own menu system, which is quite large and uses a number of submenus. For some applications such as simple photo retouching it is not necessary to resort to using layers, but they are crucial to many of the more advanced techniques that are possible using Photoshop.

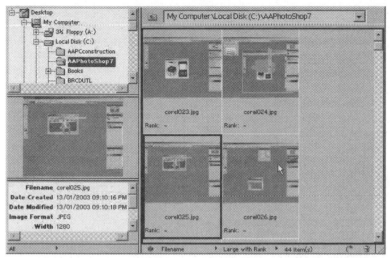

*Fig.1.32 Photoshop 7 has this alternative file browser which shows a
thumbnail view for each image file*

The Image menu is one that has already been covered to some extent,
as it is the one that contains the image and canvas resizing functions.
Further options on this menu include one to rotate the canvas and another
that permits the mode to be changed. An image can, for instance, be
converted from colour to black and white using the mode changing
function.

Adjustments submenu

A huge range of useful functions are available from the Adjustments
submenu (Figure 1.33), including such things as colour adjustment and
controls for contrast and brightness. The functions of this submenu are
used a great deal when processing digital photographs and scans. In
fact you will probably use it for every digital image that you process.
There are some automatic adjustments available, and these will often
provide a quick fix for substandard images. They do not work well with
all images though, and manual adjustment is the only way to set the
perfect contrast, colour balance, etc., for each image.

The Select menu might seem a bit pointless, since there are selection
tools available and various options for them on the Options bar. However,
the Select menu provides additional features, such as the ability to expand

1   The basics

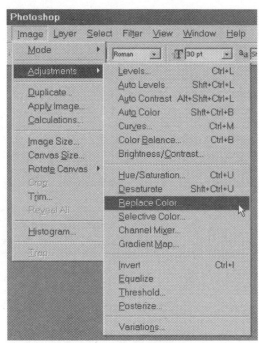

Fig.1.33 A wide range of facilities are available from the Adjustments submenu

or contract a selection by a certain number of pixels. There are tricks that help to make moved or pasted areas blend into the background more naturally. There is also an Inverse option which selects everything outside the selected area instead of everything inside it. In standard fashion, the Photoshop menu options are only active if they are usable, and inactive entries are greyed-out. In the case of the Select menu this means that practically all the options are unavailable unless there is a current selection.

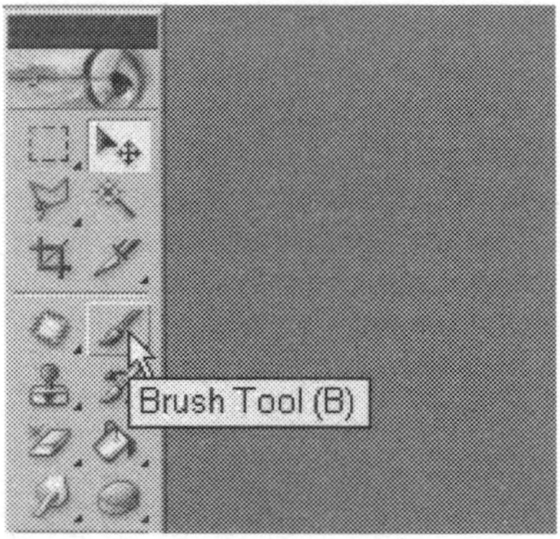

Note that Photoshop, like most programs, does have some overlap between the menus, the Toolbox, and palettes. It also has the usual range of keyboard shortcuts. The menus indicate the keyboard shortcuts, and placing the pointer over a button produces the name of the button and the keyboard shortcut (Figure 1.34). In some cases there is more than one way of achieving the same thing. A rectangular crop can be produced using the Crop tool, or selecting an area using the

Fig.1.34 One of the popup prompts for the buttons

Marquee tool and then selecting Crop from the Image menu. Where there is a choice, use whichever method you find the most convenient.

Filter menu

Various filter effects are available from the Filter menu, and some of these can be used to blur the image or increase its apparent sharpness. There are numerous other filter effects available. These can do such things as give a mosaic effect or turn the image into what looks like a drawing or an oil painting. There are various special effects to make objects "glow" or distort them, and an assortment of textures can be added. The range of effects can be extended by using two or three filters in succession, and there are hundreds of third-party filters that can be added to Photoshop. Figures 1.35 and 1.36 respectively show "before" and "after" images for a picture that has been processed using the Glass filter. With most filters there is a control panel that enables various aspects of the effect to be adjusted, including its strength.

I suppose that filters are one of those things that you love or hate. Many users make no use of them at all while others spend much of their time with Photoshop trying filter effects. It is easy to get carried away with this type of thing, but it is also a mistake to ignore this part of the program. For example, filter effects can be useful for enhancing backgrounds and making the foreground object or objects stand out. Even if you ignore the creative possibilities of filters, the sharpening filters can be very useful with photographic images that lack "bite".

View menu

The View menu has various zoom controls, which to some extent duplicate the Zoom tool in the Toolbox. There are a couple of very useful additions, and one of these is the Fit on Screen option. This makes the displayed image as large as possible within the available screen space, and gives you the biggest possible view of the complete image. The Actual Pixels option displays the image on a straightforward one image pixel per screen pixel. This lets you see exactly what the image looks like without any rounding up or rounding down errors.

If you have doubts about the sharpness of an image it is a good idea to display it using the Actual Pixels option. Viewing the whole of a high resolution image on the screen often gives the impression that it is sharper than it actually is. Zooming in at a random ratio can sometimes have the

Fig.1.35 *The original version of the image with no filtering applied*

Fig.1.36 *The "after" version of the image, with Glass filtering applied*

opposite effect. The Print Size option displays the image at approximately the size it would be printed using the current size settings.

Rulers and guides

The Rulers option enables vertical and horizontal rulers to be added to an image (Figure 1.37). A line on each ruler indicates the current cursor position. The rulers can help with the accurate placement of objects on the image, and do not forget that a co-ordinate display is available from the Info panel.

Guides are another aid to the placement of lines, text, shapes, and other objects, and It Is an extremely useful feature. Guides are simply horizontal and vertical lines that are added to an image as

Fig.1.37 Rulers added to an image

placement aids, but they do not form part of the image. To add a guide, start by going to the View menu and then select the New Guide option. This produces a small dialogue box (Figure 1.38) where two radio buttons are used to select a horizontal or vertical guide line. The position of the line can be set by entering a suitable figure in the textbox. Repeat this process to add further guide lines.

Once they are in place, guide lines can be moved to new positions by dragging them using the Move tool. Note that when the rulers are switched on, guides can be added by simply dragging them from the rulers. The

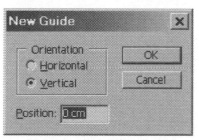

Fig.1.38 The New Guide window

Fig.1.39 Text attached to a vertical guide

orientation of a guide line can be altered by holding down the Alt key (Option key for Macs) while dragging it. Guides can be hidden by going to the View menu, selecting the Show submenu, and then selecting Guides. The guides can be toggled on and off in this way. Individual guides can be removed by dragging them off the edge of the image. Select Clear Guides from the View menu to remove all the guides.

Snap

Guides can be used as a visual aid when placing objects, but objects can also be made to snap to the guides. Various snap options are available via the Snap To submenu of the View menu. In Figure 1.39 a vertical guide has been added and some vertical text has been dragged close to the line until it snapped to the left-hand side of the guide. The text would snap to the other side of the line just as easily. With Document

Fig.1.40 Here the text has snapped to the edge of the image

Bounds ticked in the Snap To submenu, the text can also be snapped to the edge of the image, as in Figure 1.40 where it has been snapped to the right-hand edge.

There is an alternative to the guides in the form of grid lines. The grid is activated by going to the Show submenu and selecting the Grid option, and it is toggled off again by repeating this process. The grid is a regular pattern of lines, much like graph paper, that is superimposed on the image (Figure 1.41). Of course, like the guides, the grid lines do not appear when the image is printed or exported. They are there to act as placement aids and are not part of the image. Also like the guides, objects can be made to snap to the grid lines.

Try activating the grid and then draw some rectangles using the rectangular version of the Shape tool. It is possible to draw rectangles that do not adhere to the grid lines, but there is a natural tendency for the shapes to jump onto the grid lines when the pointer is placed close to them. This makes it easy to draw accurately using the snap grid feature, but it is still possible to draw "by eye" without switching off the snap

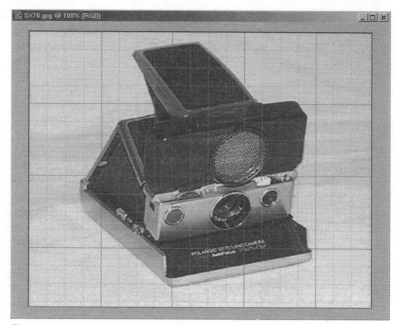

Fig.1.41 A grid of lines can be added to the image. Like the other guides, it does not appear on printed or exported images

action. It is possible to have the grid without the snap action if you simply require it as a visual drawing aid. Simply toggle off the snap action for the grid by selecting Grid from the Snap To submenu of the View menu.

Help

Last and by no means least, a comprehensive Help facility is available from the menu of the same name. The Help facility can also be activated via the standard method of operating the F1 function key. Some programs have context sensitive Help systems, where pressing F1 brings up the help screen for whatever function is being used at the time. Perhaps because it is primarily intended for professional use, Photoshop does not have context sensitive Help screens. However, the Help system has a good index and a search facility so it is not difficult to find the relevant page for a given topic.

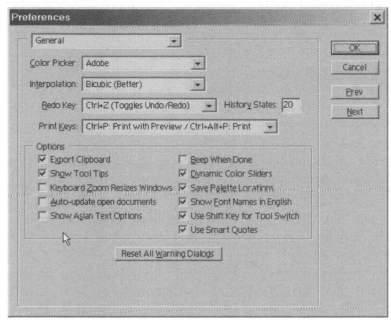

Fig.1.42 The General version of the Preferences window

Preferences

Photoshop has good customisation features, enabling users to produce a set-up that they find easy to work with. A vast number of settings can be altered via the Preferences submenu of the Edit menu. Figure 1.42 shows the General Preferences window, which is one of the seven that are available. Figure 1.43 shows the Preferences window for the display and cursors. You will need to gain some experience with Photoshop before this feature can be used really effectively, but it is worth having a quick look through the various windows to see the options that are available.

Another powerful customisation feature is the ability to move palettes from one group to another. Also, palettes located on the Options bar can be dragged into groups, and vice versa. For example, in Figure 1.44 the Navigation palette has been dragged out of its group and placed on the Options bar. In Figure 1.45 it has been dragged from the Options bar and into the Layer group of palettes. To relocate a palette, drag it by

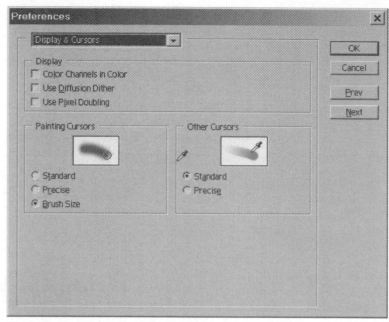

Fig.1.43 The Display and Cursors Preferences window

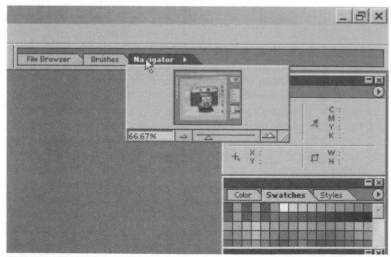

Fig.1.44 The Navigation palette has been dragged to the Options bar

the tab, and place the tab in amongst the tabs of the destination group. The outline of the palette will change when it has properly latched onto the new group. If a palette is dragged out of one group and is not placed in a new group, it will operate in its own floating window.

Experiment

Some of the tools and facilities in Photoshop are easy to use while others need a certain amount of know-how in order to get them to

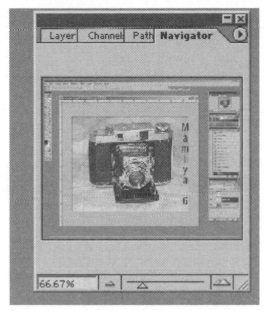

Fig.1.45 Here the Navigation palette has been dragged to another group

do anything. It is a good idea to create a blank page using the New command and then try doodling with the drawing and painting tools. You can then try some of the editing commands, adding grids and using the snap facilities, etc. I would definitely recommend experimenting with the basic brush tool and a range of brushes. Try a few variations such as the airbrush option and different Flow settings. It is much easier to progress with any program if you are comfortable with its basic facilities and its general method of operation. Some experience gained while experimenting with the program can make life much easier later on.

Points to remember

Photoshop has the usual menu bar at the top of the screen, and this provides a huge range of facilities. However, it is the Toolbox on the left-hand side of the screen that provides most of the painting, drawing, and editing facilities. You need to be familiar with the tools and the menu system in order to use Photoshop properly.

The Options bar is context sensitive, and changes to suit whatever tool is selected at the time. The available options greatly enhance the capabilities of most tools, and it is important to familiarise yourself with the extra facilities provided by the Options bar.

A huge range of functions are available from the palettes down the right-hand side of the screen, and via the tabs on the Options bar. These are used for such things as mixing and choosing colours, undoing and redoing the up to the last 20 operations carried out on an image, and controlling layers. The palettes can be dragged from one group to another, used independently as floating windows, or docked on the Options bar.

The selection tools are an important part of Photoshop. Colour changes, Copy and Paste operations, resizing, etc., can be applied to a selected part of the image. In fact it is possible to select several parts of the image and process them simultaneously. Several types of selection tool are available, and these can be used one after the other in order to add to and subtract from selections.

Photoshop can be used to resize an image in a variety of ways. For example, it can reduce the number of pixels in a high definition image so that it can be used in a web page. It can also increase the number of pixels so that a relatively low resolution image does not have excessively large pixels when printed. Remember that detail is lost when the pixel count is reduced, but no detail is added when it is boosted.

Brush tools are central to retouching photographic images. An ordinary brush can be used to "paint" onto an image, but the Clone, Patch and

Healing tools are far better for retouching photographs. These use material from elsewhere on the image, or from another image, to cover unwanted objects or blemishes on an image.

There brush style tools that can be used to do such things as sharpen, lighten, or darken parts of an image. However, most processing of this type is applied to the entire image via the menu system. In particular, the Adjustments submenu of the Image menu provides a large range of facilities for controlling contrast, colour balance, and colour saturation. In general it is better to get the image as a whole adjusted correctly before applying any selective processing.

A substantial list of filter effects is available from the Filter menu and its numerous submenus. It is definitely a case of "all your Christmases coming at once" if you are into special effects. Only the Sharpen and Blur filters will be of frequent use if you are not.

Various grids, rulers, and guides are available to help with the accurate positioning of objects (lines, text, etc.) on an image. Selections will also snap to guides.

There is only one way to learn the ins and outs of a program like Photoshop, and that is to spend time using it. Load some images and try the tools, colour balance controls, and so on. Try the techniques explained in this book with copies of your own images.

1   The basics

Ins and outs

Sources

On the face of it, opening and saving files using Photoshop is much the same as using any other program, and the usual file browser is available for both types of operation. As we saw in chapter 1, Photoshop has an alternative file browser that shows a thumbnail view of each image file, making it easy to find the right one. In many ways opening and saving files is the same as using other programs, but matters tend to be a bit more complicated when using practically any graphics program.

The problems are mainly centred on the various file formats that are used for digital images. A graphics program could use its own file format and refuse to load or save images using any other format, but it would be of relatively little use. To be of maximum value it is necessary for a program like Photoshop to be able to load images from a wide range of sources.

Bear in mind that although it is possible to produce images by "painting" them using Photoshop, it is not often used in this way. As the Photoshop name implies, its primary role is in processing photographic images from scanners, digital cameras, downloaded from the Internet, or whatever. The more sources the program can accommodate, the greater the likelihood of it handling all your image processing tasks.

Similarly, the more file formats that can be used when saving images, the more use the program is likely to be. The ability to save files in various formats is admittedly of little importance if you simply wish to process images and then print them out. However, many users need to produce image files that can be used in web pages, exported to desktop publishing programs, etc. The image files in this book for example, were obtained using Corel Capture 11, loaded into Photoshop 7, and then after processing they were exported to PageMaker 7. One of the main uses of Photoshop is in this sort of "middle man" application.

Open or Import?

There are two basic means of getting images loaded into Photoshop. The first is to use the Open command in the File menu or the Photoshop file browser to load files that are stored on a disc drive. These could be files you have downloaded from the Internet or a digital camera and stored on the hard drive, or perhaps they are files obtained on a CD-ROM. It does not really matter, because they are all loaded into Photoshop in much the same way. Photoshop can accommodate a wide range of file formats, so it is not necessary for the files to be in Photoshop's own format. On the other hand, files must be in one of the standard formats that are supported by Photoshop.

The alternative method is to import images. With some programs the Open command is used to load files in the program's own file format, with one or two other formats also being catered for. The Import command is used to load files in additional formats, which are converted to the programs own file type. Photoshop uses the Open command to load files in any compatible format, and the Import command is primarily used for bringing in images from a scanner or a digital camera. This is normally achieved using a TWAIN driver that effectively merges the camera or scanner software into Photoshop, so that image files can be downloaded directly into Photoshop.

Formats

In order to open an image using Photoshop it must be in one of the common image file formats. The various file formats do not just use different ways of storing the same information. What is stored varies somewhat from one format to another. It is helpful to have a basic understanding of the characteristics of the main file formats, so brief descriptions of them are provided here.

GIF

The full name for this format is CompuServe Graphics Interchange Format, and programs that use it have to be licensed by CompuServe. This format is generally preferred for line art such as graphs and most diagrams, or practically any non-photographic images. In fact the GIF image format is sometimes used for monochrome photographs, but these days Jpeg is the more popular choice for images of this type. With suitable images it combines small file sizes and high quality. Operation with up to 256 colours is supported, and these can be any colours rather than those from a predetermined set. No compression is used with this format, but the file sizes are kept small by the inherently compact method of storing images. An advantage of this system is that images are produced in high quality on high-resolution printers, etc. The higher the resolution of the output device, the higher the quality of reproduction that is achieved with line art images. Bitmap images, unless very large numbers of pixels are used, produce rather chunky looking results when printed large. This format is suitable for web applications. GIF files can be used for simple animations incidentally.

Jpeg or Jpg

Whether called Jpeg or Jpg, it is pronounced jay-peg. This is now the most common format used for bit maps. A bitmap is an image that is made up of dots, or pixels as they are termed. A computer monitor produces images in this fashion, and any type of graphic can be represented as a bitmap. However, it produces large files and often gives relatively poor results when applied to line drawings. This file format is mainly used with photographic images, or pseudo photographic images, where it enables good results to be obtained without resorting to large file sizes. The modest file size is achieved using compression. With some programs, including Photoshop, you can use varying degrees of compression and up to three different types.

Note that the small file sizes obtained when using high degrees of compression are obtained at the expense of reduced picture quality. In Internet applications it is clearly helpful to have small files in order to keep download times to a minimum. On the other hand, there is no point in having an image that downloads quickly if no one can see what it is meant to be! The borderline between acceptable and unacceptable quality is a subjective matter, and can only be determined using the "suck it and see" approach.

Figure 2.1 shows a photograph that has been saved in Jpeg format using minimal compression, and Figure 2.2 shows the same photograph with maximum compression. These produce file sizes of about 900k and 100k respectively, and there is surprisingly little difference between them. However, with a colour image any artefacts added by the compression tend to be more noticeable, so this monochrome image is perhaps overstating the case for using large amounts of compression. However, it does demonstrate the fact that large amounts of compression do not necessarily produce very poor quality.

Fig.2.1 At about 900k this Jpeg image has minimal compression

Png

This is a relatively new file format for images, and it is apparently pronounced pong, as in nasty smell or Ping-Pong. Png stands for Portable Network Graphic. It is designed to be a sort of universal license-free image format that will eventually replace the GIF format. It combines small file sizes with the ability to use an unlimited colour range. Although relatively new, any reasonably modern browser should be able to handle Png images (Internet Explorer 4 or later for example). However, it is less universal than either the Jpg or GIF formats.

TIFF or TIF

TIFF (Tagged Image File Format) is one of the older image file formats, and it stores images as bitmaps. It is sometimes called TIF rather than TIFF, and files of this type usually have TIF as the extension to the filename.

Fig.2.2 Even compressed to about 100k the quality is quite good

Although popular at one time, it has to some extent given way to Jpg files which offer smaller file sizes. It is still quite popular for use with desktop publishing programs though. There is also an Enhanced TIFF format that supports layers, but this might give compatibility problems with some programs.

EPS

Encapsulated Postscript is another format that is mainly used in desktop publishing. However, it is primarily used for charts and diagrams rather than photographic images. Unless very high resolution is used, bitmaps often give disappointing results when used with anything more than simple charts and diagrams. EPS should give high quality results provided the source material is "up to scratch", but the file sizes can be quite large.

BMP

This is a simple bitmap format, and judging from the file sizes produced using this format, no compression is used. It is the standard Windows bitmap format, and should be supported by any Windows graphics program.

PDF

This is the Adobe portable document format, and it is a cross-platform format. PDF is actually a general-purpose file format that can handle text and any type of image. This book was sent to the printers in the form of a single PDF file for example. A high degree of compression is used, but results of excellent quality are produced. Adobe Acrobat reader is needed to view PDF files, but the reader program is free from the Adobe web site and is available for several types of computer and various operating systems. The popular web browsers link to the reader program so that they can effectively be used to display PDF documents. This format is a popular choice for complex and (or) large documents, but it can be used with single images.

PICT

Files that use this format normally have PIC as the extension. This is a Macintosh format that is mainly used in desktop publishing. Many Windows programs support this graphics format, including the Windows version of Photoshop.

PCX

This is an early bitmap format that was very popular at one time. Not surprising really, since there was little competition in those days. It is not used very much now, but you might have or obtain some old image files in this format.

RAW

Not exactly a file format in the conventional sense, it is more a means of importing and exporting images. It is used a great deal with the more upmarket digital cameras as a means of uploading images with the highest possible quality. In other words, the raw image data is exported with no compression or file conversion.

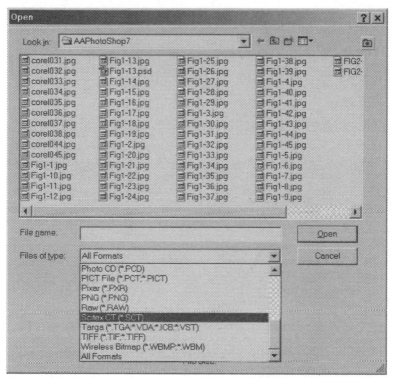

Fig.2.3 The file browser can be restricted to displaying files of one particular format

PSD

This is Photoshop's native format, and it can obviously handle anything that Photoshop itself can handle (text, layers, etc.). Relatively few programs can import or export in this form, so although it is Photoshop's native format, you will not necessarily use it very much. In fact many users do not bother with this format at all. If you use this format to export images to another program, bear in mind that some of the fancier features available from Photoshop might not be carried through to the other program. Transparency information can be lost for example.

There are other graphics file formats in use, but the ones described in the previous section are the only ones you are likely to use with Photoshop. By default, the Photoshop file browser will show all compatible graphics files when opening images. The File of type menu

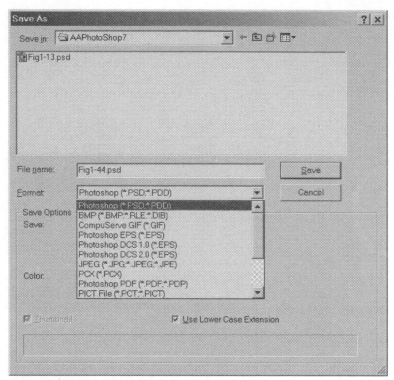

Fig.2.4 Images can be saved in a number of common formats

(Figure 2.3) can be used to restrict the browser to files of one particular type. There is a similar menu available in the Save As file browser (Figure 2.4), and this can be used to change the format in which the image file is saved.

With some images you might find that only a limited range of file formats is available when saving them. This occurs when the image contains something that certain file formats can not handle. In practice this usually occurs because the image has two or more layers, and relatively few formats support layer information. It is possible to get around this by merging layers or using the Flatten Image command on the Layers menu. However, bear in mind that once the layer information is lost it can not be retrieved. Where necessary, flatten the image so that it can be exported to another program, but keep a copy of the original image file, complete with all the layer information.

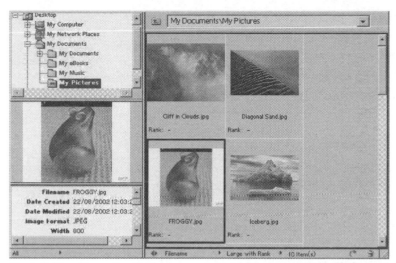

Fig.2.5 The alternative file browser shows a thumbnail for each image file in the selected folder

File Browser

Files are opened in the standard fashion using the Open command in the File menu. In some cases Photoshop might not be able to determine the file format of an image. This could be due to it having a non-standard file extension for example. The Open As option can then be used, with the correct file type being selected from the menu. The File Browser panel is significantly different to the standard browser (Figure 2.5). The top left-hand section is used to select the correct folder in the usual way. The bottom section on this side shows some information about the selected file, such as its name, date of creation, and size. The amount of information varies somewhat, depending on the type of file and its source.

The main section of the window shows a thumbnail picture for each graphics file in the selected folder. The central panel on the left shows a slightly larger thumbnail of the selected file. In most cases there will be far too many thumbnails to fit into the main section of the window, but you can scroll through the pictures using the scrollbar. It is possible to use the entire window to show the thumbnail views (Figure 2.6). It is just a matter of operating the small button in the bar at the bottom of the window, just to the left of the word "Filename". The division between the

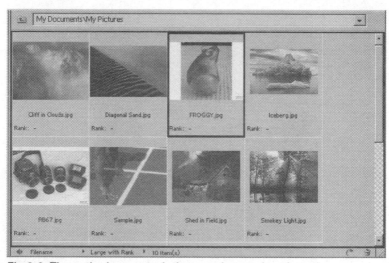

My Documents\My Pictures

Cliff in Clouds.jpg   Diagonal Sand.jpg   FROGGY.jpg   Iceberg.jpg
Rank: -   Rank: -   Rank: -   Rank: -

RB67.jpg   Sample.jpg   Shed in Field.jpg   Smokey Light.jpg
Rank: -   Rank: -   Rank: -   Rank: -

Filename   Large with Rank   10 item(s)

Fig.2.6 The entire browser window can be used to show the thumbnails of the files

two sides of the window can be dragged to a new position, so it can be moved to the right to give more space to the browser section for example.

The button at the right end of the bar deletes the selected file, but only after you have confirmed the deletion. The button just to the left of this rotates the image 90 degrees in a clockwise direction, or counter-clockwise if the Alt (or Option) key is held down while operating the button. A popup message (Figure 2.7) explains that only the thumbnail picture is rotated unless the image is opened. Until then the image file remains

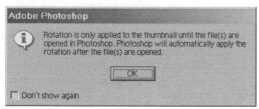

Adobe Photoshop

Rotation is only applied to the thumbnail until the file(s) are opened in Photoshop. Photoshop will automatically apply the rotation after the file(s) are opened.

OK

☐ Don't show again

Fig.2.7 Only the thumbnail is rotated unless the file is opened

unchanged. It is advisable to tick the Don't show again checkbox to suppress further appearances of this message.

Right-clicking on an image produces the useful popup menu of Figure 2.8. This permits images to be opened, rotated, renamed, or deleted. It is also possible to open an image by double-clicking on its thumbnail, or where applicable, the enlarged thumbnail in the left-hand section of the window. The Select All option, as one would expect, selects al the image files in the folder, and Deselect All reverses this operation.

Photoshop can have a number of open images, but only if the computer has sufficient memory to accommodate them all. Multiple images can be individually selected in the usual way, which in the case of a Windows system means holding down

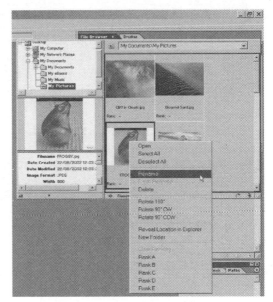

Fig.2.8 A popup menu is available

the Control key and left-clicking each of the required images. The same method deselects an image that is already selected. In order to open multiple images, either double-click on one of them or right-click on one and select Open from the popup menu.

Associations

In addition to opening a file from within Photoshop it possible to open a suitable file by double-clicking on its entry in any file browser, such as Windows Explorer. There are a few "strings attached" though, and with a Macintosh computer the file must be one that has Photoshop listed as the file creator. In a Windows set-up, the file will be opened using whatever program is associated with that particular file type. If there is more than one graphics program installed on the PC, it is possible that some compatible graphics formats will not be associated with Photoshop. If necessary, this can be altered by changing the relevant Windows file associations. If it is not already running, opening an associated file will automatically launch Photoshop.

Conversion

Since Photoshop can load and save files in a range of formats, it can be used to provide file conversion. For example, suppose that you have a TIFF file and you need to convert it to a Jpeg type for use in a web application. Just load the file into Photoshop and then use the Save As function to save it as a Jpeg file. This generates the required Jpeg file and leaves the original TIFF file unchanged.

Bear in mind that any file conversion can produce some odd results, and that graphics files are more difficult to convert than most other types. In the past, most types of graphics conversion were virtually guaranteed to scramble the image slightly, or even totally. Fortunately, things are better these days. Photoshop generally does a very good job, and there should be few problems when converting from one bitmap format to another. Layers and other fancy features can be more difficult to convert, and may not be supported by the output file type. Some processing of the image may then be needed before the conversion can be made, and compromises may have to be accepted.

Importing

Some digital cameras and scanners are supplied with software that downloads the pictures to the hard disc and stores them in one of the popular file formats. The images can then be opened using Photoshop. The more usual method is to have a special driver such as a TWAIN type that permits images to be downloaded directly into Photoshop, or any other program that supports this method of importation. Both methods are perfectly usable, but I think it is fair to say that most users prefer to load images directly into Photoshop.

It is important to realise that Photoshop has no built-in ability to read images direct from a piece of hardware such as a digital camera or a scanner. In order to do this it requires the services of a Photoshop compatible plug-in or other add-on software. Most scanners and digital cameras are supplied with a TWAIN driver, Photoshop plug-in, or some other software to permit direct importation into Photoshop. Without this software it is not possible to import images directly into Photoshop.

Methods for installing the software vary depending on its exact type. These days most pieces or hardware are supplied complete with an installation disc that automatically installs the drivers and any other software supplied with the device. In some cases it is necessary to copy one or more files to the appropriate folder on the hard disc. Always follow the manufacturer's installation instructions "to the letter".

Note that in some cases it will be necessary to restart the computer before the driver software becomes active. If plug-in files have to be copied to a folder on the hard disc it is normally recommended that this should not be done with Photoshop running. It does not usually matter too much if Photoshop is running when the files are copied, but the program will probably have to be closed and restarted before the plug-in or plug-ins will become active.

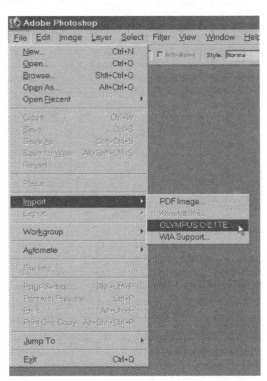

With everything set up and switched on, importing starts by selecting Import from the File menu, and then selecting the required source from the submenu. In the example of Figure 2.9 the required source is an Olympus digital camera that is using a TWAIN driver. Note that with older versions of Photoshop it might be necessary to select the TWAIN source

Fig.2.9 Selecting the source when importing images from a piece of hardware

first, and where appropriate there will be a separate submenu for this purpose. The TWAIN drive is then activated by selecting the TWAIN or TWAIN32 option from the Import submenu.

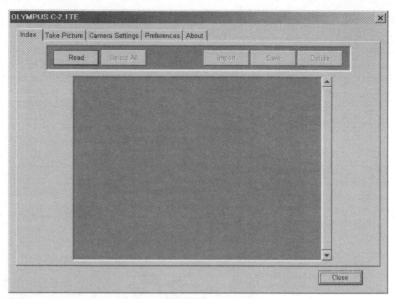

Fig.2.10 *The downloader for the Olympus camera. Each hardware device has its own downloader program*

Selecting files

What happens next depends on the software that is interfacing the hardware to Photoshop. The software used to select and download images is different for each device. Some cameras use a plug-in that makes use of the Photoshop File Browser, and the images are then imported much like opening image files on a disc drive. In this case the window of Figure 2.10 appeared when the Olympus camera was selected from the Import submenu.

The first task is to operate the Read button so that thumbnails of the pictures in the camera are displayed (Figure 2.11). Files are selected in much the same way as using the Photoshop File Browser, and then they are loaded into Photoshop by operating the Import button. Figure 2.12 shows one of the photographs successfully downloaded into Photoshop. There will usually be further features available from the downloader program, and in this case it is possible to delete selected images in the camera, save images directly to disc, and adjust various camera settings.

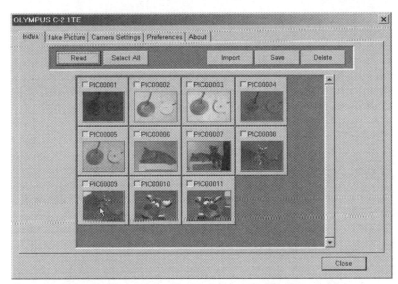

Fig.2.11 Thumbnail views for the images stored in the camera

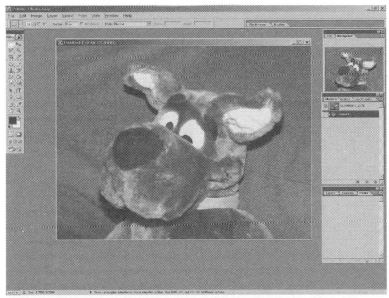

Fig.2.12 One of the images successfully downloaded to Photoshop

With (say) a flatbed scanner, the facilities offered by the downloader would obviously be somewhat different. There would be a preview mode to produce a thumbnail of the scanned image, and facilities to crop the image at source. There might also be contrast, brightness and colour controls, but most users probably prefer to handle this type of this once the image has been loaded into Photoshop. The controls available in Photoshop are likely to be much better than those provided by the scanning utility. Anyway, it should not take too long to master the basics of importing images into Photoshop.

Save As Copy

Once loaded into Photoshop, the images are unlikely to be in Photoshop's own PSD format. It is more likely that they will be in a popular bitmap format such as TIFF or Jpeg. However, they can be saved in PSD or one of the other output formats supported by Photoshop, so the initial format is not of too much importance. It is not a bad idea save each image twice using slightly different names such as Beachscene_1 and Beachscene_2. You can then have an untouched original version of the image and one that can be freely processed.

If things should go horribly wrong with the processed image and the History facility does not allow things to be sufficiently undone, you can always go back to the original image and try again. Actually, a snapshot is added at the top of the History palette when an image is loaded, and it is possible to revert to this at any time by left-clicking on the snapshot. However, the original snapshot will be lost if the image is saved and reloaded.

A big advantage of digital imaging is that you can save different versions of the image under separate names, and have as many variations as you like. Disc storage space is relatively cheap these days so it costs very little to store images on a hard disc or CD-R discs. Always keep a copy of the original version so that you have the option of going right back to the beginning should you wish to do so.

In addition to the usual Save and Save As options in the File menu, Photoshop has a Save As Copy option. If the Save As function is used to save an image under a new name, it is that new version of the file that becomes the current one. Any further processing is applied to that version of the file. With the Save As Copy function, the current image is saved under a new name, but any further processing is applied to the original copy of the file. The general idea is that you can use the Save As Copy

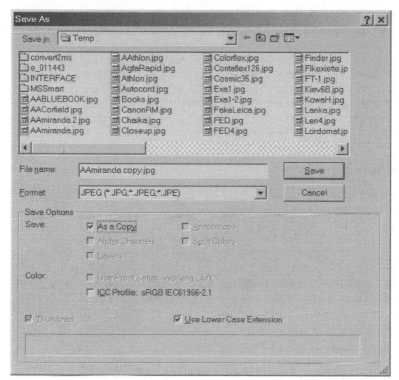

Fig.2.13 The Save As facility is available via a checkbox in the standard Save As window

function to save a copy of the image under a new name before starting work on it. You can then use this command again, each time you have a new version that you wish to save.

In order to use the Save As Copy function the Save As option is selected from the File menu. This produces the dialogue box of Figure 2.13. The file will be saved as a copy if the As a copy checkbox is ticked. The filename will have "copy" added at the end, but the name can be edited to any name you prefer. Of course, the new name must be different to the one used for the original copy of the file.

There is also a Save for Web option in the File menu, and this produces the Window of Figure 2.14. This offers various settings that enable the image to be optimised for web use. The size can be altered, varying degrees of compression can be applied, as can a blur effect, and so on.

Fig.2.14 The Save for Web option produces this window

The preview image enables you to view the effects of any changes that are made.

Oops

When using practically any computer program it is a good idea to regularly save your work so that there is always a recent copy to go back to if there is a power failure, a system crash, or the computer is accidentally reset. Another reason for frequently saving work is that you can then go back to a previous version if you make a complete mess of an image. As pointed out previously, this is not really necessary with Photoshop, since there is a multi-level Undo/Redo facility available from the Edit menu, and from Photoshop 5 onwards there is a more sophisticated version available from the History palette.

The latter is something that all Photoshop users need to be familiar with at an early stage. The History palette makes it possible to freely experiment with images, happy in the knowledge that it is possible to go

Fig.2.15 This image has undergone a number of processes

back a number of stages at the click of a mouse if you change your mind. Figure 2.15 shows the screen with an image that has undergone several stages of processing. The History palette can be seen to the right of the image, and it lists the various changes that have been made to the image, right back to when it was opened.

There is a brief description of each operation, such as Rotate Canvas or Sharpen, making it easy to go back to the required stage in the processing. Simply left-click on the appropriate entry in the History palette in order to go back to that stage of the processing. In Figure 2.16 the image has been taken back to the first change that was made. It is possible to jump backward and forward as much as you like to any desired states in the list.

Buttons

The three buttons at the bottom of the History palette provide some useful features. Working from left to right, the first of them creates a new

Fig.2.16 The processing has been instantly reversed via the
        History palette

document using the current stage as the starting point. You can therefore
jump back to an earlier stage and try again from there, leaving the original
version fully intact. Bear in mind that going back to an earlier stage and
continuing to edit from there effectively deletes the changes that were
undone. With them gone from the History palette they are no longer
available.

The next button creates a new snapshot of the image at its current state.
This snapshot appears near the top of the list of changes (Figure 2.17),
and can be selected just like any of the other entries in the list. This can
provide a "get out clause" if you go back to an earlier stage, start editing
from there, and then decide you preferred your previous effort. Take a
snapshot before going back and redoing the editing. If you change your
mind it is just a matter of clicking the snapshot in order to revert to the
previous editing, and there is no need to save a new version of the image
to disc.

The snapshot facility is also useful because Photoshop has a limit of 20
changes in the History palette. Therefore, after a while, each new change

results in an earlier one being deleted from the beginning of the list. This is done in order to prevent the History palette from using too much memory. Using the snapshot facility it is possible to jump back to strategic points in the development of the image, even if those points no longer appear in the list of changes.

It is possible to delete the selected state, and all subsequent ones, by operating the third button. You will be asked to confirm that you wish to make the deletions, so there is a chance to change your mind before obliterating a series of changes. This change is also reversible via the Undo facility if you should change your mind.

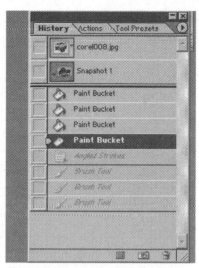

Fig.2.17 A snapshot has been added to the palette

It is important to realise that the History palette has one or two limitations. As already pointed out, it only stores the last 20 changes, so there is a limit to how much you can undo. Even things like selecting an area using the Marquee tool, or deselecting it, count as changes. The 20 changes can soon be used up. Another limitation to keep in mind is that the History palette is not saved with images. Consequently, it is not possible to undo changes that were made in a previous session working on that image. If you might need to rework images from earlier stages, make sure that you save separate copies of the image at each of those stages.

Which format

With so many formats available using Photoshop, which one should be used? Unless there is good reason to do otherwise, it is probably best to keep the image in whatever format it happens to be in when loaded into Photoshop. In practice there will often be good reasons to use a different format. If you import a Jpeg image from a digital camera and wish to make prints from it or use it in a web page, there is no obvious reason for using a different format.

Fig.2.18 This flattened Jpeg image looks no different to the two-layer PSD version

However, if you use some of the more advanced facilities available in Photoshop you may be forced into a change to the PSD format. Adding text on new layers for example, will make it impossible to save the image using a simple bitmap format such as Jpeg, which does not support layers. With complex images such as multi-layer types it is advisable to use Photoshop's own PSD format. Flatten the images and save them in Jpeg format if they are eventually needed for web pages or another application that requires this format. Alternatively, just save them in Jpeg format and Photoshop will automatically flatten the saved images.

Make sure that the PSD versions are retained though. It is not possible to reverse the flattening process, and editing of a flattened image is likely to be relatively difficult. Editing will be much easier if you can revert to a PSD version that is complete with layer information. Figure 2.18 shows a two-layer image that has been saved in Jpeg format. The image was on one layer and the text was on another. There is no obvious difference between the look of the original and flattened image, which for all practical purposes are the same in this respect. There is an important difference in that the text in the layered version can be freely moved and edited without altering the rest of the image. This is not the case with the flattened version, where the text has effectively become part of the image.

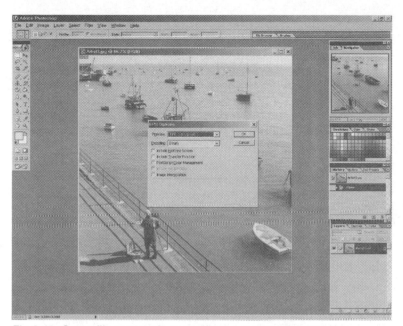

Fig.2.19 Some file conversions produce a popup dialogue box

Jpeg is the most widely used format for web applications, and it is also used a great deal in desktop publishing. It is not well suited to all web applications though, and it is primarily for photographic images. It often gives poor results with images such as charts and diagrams in a line art format, and GIF is a better choice for publishing this type of thing on the web. EPS is usually a better choice for line art that is used in desktop publishing. When converting to some formats, including EPS, a dialogue box like the one in Figure 2.19 will appear. Sensible defaults are used, so it is only necessary to alter the settings if the converted images are not as expected.

Accuracy

In the case of desktop publishing it is usually best to try all the compatible formats to determine which one works best. Diagrams often lose something in the translation, or gain something, so experiment to find a format that gives consistently accurate results. Pay particular attention to any text. Text is usually problem-free when converting from one bitmap format to another, but with other types of conversion it can shift or change in size relative to the rest of the image.

EPS often provides the most accurate results, but you have to put up with large file sizes when using this format. The same is true of the TIFF bitmap format, which can be used as an alternative to Jpeg with many desktop publishing programs. Using a modest amount of compression it is possible to obtain similar results using Jpeg, but with image files that are about 80 to 90 percent smaller. Where there is a choice of these two formats I would certainly opt for Jpeg rather than TIFF files.

If it is necessary to export an image to another graphics program, PICT (Macintosh) and BMP (Windows) are popular choices. BMP is a straightforward bitmap format that should give accurate results, and should be compatible with any Windows program that can handle bitmaps. Again, file sizes are quite big with this format, which does not use any form of file compression. Windows has another standard image file format in the form of Windows Metafiles (WMF format). However, Photoshop can not open or save images in this format.

It is not a good idea to search for a universal format that will give good results in any application and with any type of image. Possibly such a format will exist one day, but at the moment there is no single format that will give perfect results in any application, and that is compatible with every program. Be prepared to experiment with various file formats and use the one that gives the best overall results in each application.

Printing

Printing from Photoshop direct to your own laser printer, inkjet, etc., can be much like printing out from any other program. On the other hand, Photoshop has a lot optional extras available, should you need them. The simple way to print from Photoshop is to Select the Print option from the File menu, which will produce the usual Print dialogue box. A warning message like the one in Figure 2.20 will appear first if the image

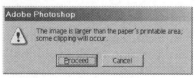

Fig.2.20 This warning appears if the image is too large

is too large to fit the paper. It is possible to go ahead without taking any remedial action, but only part of the image will be printed.

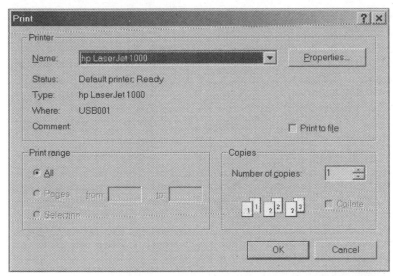

Fig.2.21 Make sure the correct printer is selected in the Print window

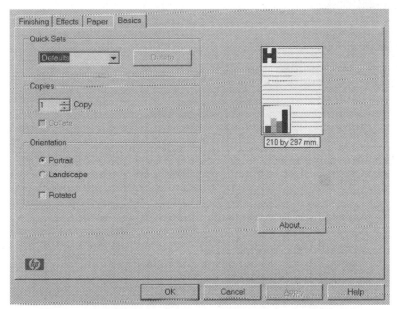

Fig.2.22 The orientation can be set in the Printer Properties window

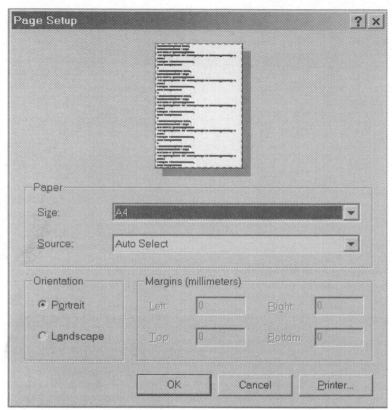

*Fig.2.23 The Page Setup window. This varies somewhat from one
        printer to another*

This warning can occur because the size of the image has been
misjudged, or you have simply forgotten to set a suitable size for that
picture. In most cases though, it is because the image is in landscape
format and the printer is set to portrait mode. One solution is to operate
the Cancel button, rotate the image through 90 degrees, and then select
the Print command again. The image can be restored to its previous
orientation once it has been printed.

Alternatively, operate the Proceed button and change the mode of the
printer from the Print dialogue box (Figure 2.21). Make sure that the
correct printer is selected in the Name menu if there is more than one

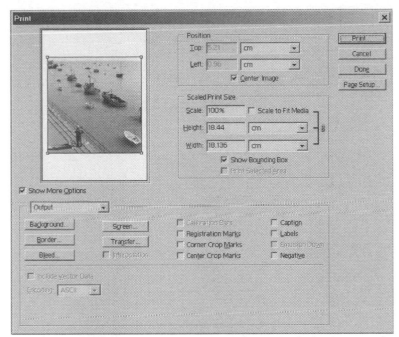

Fig.2.24 The Print with Preview window provides numerous adjustments and options

printer connected to your PC. Operating the Properties button will bring up the dialogue box for the appropriate printer. This is different for each printer, but one of the windows should enable the orientation of the printer to be set (Figure 2.22). Having set the correct orientation, operate the Apply button and then the OK button to return to the Print dialogue box, and then operate the OK button to go ahead and print the page.

The better way of handling things is to use the Page Setup facility that is available from the File menu. This window is another one that is different for each printer, and the one shown in Figure 2.23 is for my HP LaserJet 1000 printer. The facilities will vary from one printer to another, but as a minimum it should be possible to set the paper size, source, and orientation. The advantage of this method is that it only controls the settings used for Photoshop. The printer's default settings remain unaltered and will be used by other programs.

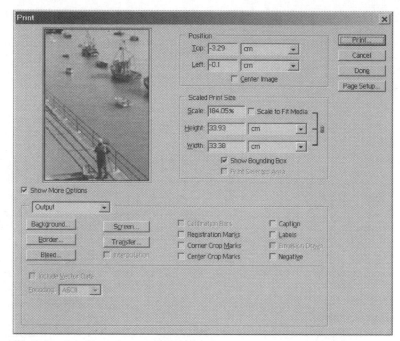

Fig.2.25 A selected part of the image can be made to fill the page

Print with Preview

There is an even better way of handling things in the form of the Print with Preview option, which is again available under the File menu. This produces the dialogue box of Figure 2.24. The paper size and orientation can be set via the Page Setup button, and there are numerous facilities available from the dialogue box itself. For example, a black border up to 3.5 millimetres wide can be added to the image, and the normally white background colour can be replaced with another colour. The Color Picker appears so that the required colour can be chosen.

The image can be scaled up or down by dragging the four handles or the edges of the thumbnail view. With the tick removed from the Centre Image checkbox it is also possible to drag the image around the paper. Any desired part of the image can be made to fill the printable part of the paper, as in the example of Figure 2.25. Alternatively, the textboxes enable

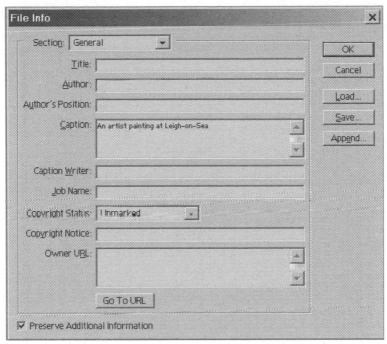

Fig.2.26 A caption can be added via the File Info window

an exact size, scale, and position to be specified for the printed image. Place a tick in the Scale to Fit Media checkbox if you simply need to print the image as large as possible. There are various options for printing registration and crop marks, printing the image as a negative, and so on. Many of these options are only used with professional printing equipment and services, and are of little use with personal printers.

With the Labels option selected the filename is printed above the image. Of course, sufficient space must be left above the image, and you can see from the preview panel whether the label will print properly. A caption will be printed below the image if the Caption checkbox is ticked. Of course, this only works if a caption has been added, and this is done by selecting the File Info option from the File menu. This produces the dialogue box of Figure 2.26, where the required text is typed into the Caption textbox. Figure 2.27 shows the scan of a printout that has a 3.5 millimetre border, a label, a caption, registration marks, and corner crop marks.

Fig.2.27 This scan of a printout has a 3.5 millimetre border, registration marks, corner crop marks, a label, and a caption

Points to remember

Photoshop has its own PSD format, and the advantage of using this one is that it can handle layers, transparency levels, etc. Photoshop can use several other image file formats, including most of the popular ones for use with Macintosh computers and PCs. It will often be necessary to resort to one of these formats in order to export images to desktop publishing programs or use them on the Internet.

Bear in mind that many file formats do not support layers or some of the other facilities available using Photoshop. Any layer information, etc., is lost when images are saved in one of these formats. Save an image in PSD format first if you would like to retain this information, which can make life easier if you need to undertake further editing at some later time.

The ordinary Save and Open commands are used when saving or opening image files, even if they are not in Photoshop's own PSD format. The Import command is used to download images from a piece of hardware such as a digital camera or a scanner. It is only possible to import images if the appropriate driver, such as a TWAIN type, has been installed on the computer.

Files can be opened via the standard file browser, and this shows a thumbnail view of the currently selected image. An alternative file browser is available by operating the appropriate tab on the Options bar. This represents each file by a thumbnail image, which makes life easier if you do not know the name of the file you wish to open.

It is possible to have several images open in Photoshop, but bear in mind that several high resolution images will require large amounts of memory.

The History palette makes it possible to instantly go back up to 20 steps, so it is easy to undo processing that has gone awry. Bear in mind that going back a number of steps and working from there deletes the steps that have been retraced, so you can not change your mind again.

A snapshot of the current image can be taken by operating the appropriate button at the bottom of the History palette. The snapshot is added at the top of the palette, and it is possible to restore the image to that state at any time simply by left-clicking on the snapshot. Note though, that snapshots are not saved with the image. Any snapshots you wish to preserve must be saved as separate files.

There is no universal image file format that is suitable for all applications. If you use Photoshop to prepare images for the Internet, for professional printing, for desktop publishing, etc., it will probably be necessary to use several file types.

For the maximum flexibility and facilities, use the Print with Preview option when producing printouts from Photoshop. Amongst other things, this provides a small WYSIWYG (what you see is what you get) preview of the printout.

Making selections

Selective processing

Getting images into and out of Photoshop is easy enough, but how do you go about processing the images to obtain really professional results? Some processing is applied to the entire image, such as brightening an image that is underexposed and too dark. Other processing has to be selective. Suppose that you have an image of an object such as a piece of jewellery, and it is on a rather uninspiring background. You might decide to paint in a simple graduated background instead of the original. This type of thing is much used in advertising, where the main subject is made to look more dynamic and stand out better by replacing the natural background. It can be used to good effect if you produce photographs for online auctions or something of this type.

Having to carefully paint around a complex object is very time consuming. It would clearly be much easier if there was a way of selecting the outline of the main subject and setting everything within it as a no-go area. It would then be easy to paint on the background using the brush tools or using flood fills, as there would be no danger of altering the main subject. Indeed, even if you tried to paint over the main subject it would not be possible to do so.

The Photoshop selection tools provide various means of selecting areas that can either be used as no-go zones or the only areas that can be altered. It is only fair to point out that selecting precisely the right part of an image can be quite easy or very difficult depending on the nature of the image. Something that has "hard" edges that contrast well with the background is likely to be easier than something that has "soft" edges with a tendency to blend into the background. Photoshop has tools and functions that help to deal with awkward parts of an image, but there is no guarantee of perfect results every time. With uncooperative images it is necessary to draw at least part of the selection outline by hand.

In order to increase the chances of selecting exactly the required areas, Photoshop has several selection tools that operate in different ways. The Marquee tools are the most basic, and the rectangular Marquee tool simply selects the area within a rectangle dragged onto the screen. Although it is a pretty basic method of selection, it is one that you will probably use a fair amount in real-world image processing. The Marquee can be restricted to a square by holding down the Shift key while dragging it onto the screen.

Alternatives

There is an elliptical version of the Marquee tool which no doubt has its uses, but it is probably not something that will be used frequently. Note that a circle will be produced if the Shift key is held down while using the Elliptical Marquee tool.

There are two more versions of the Marquee tool, which are the Single Column and Single Row varieties. These respectively select a complete vertical column of pixels and a complete horizontal row of pixels. Again, this is probably not the type of thing you will require every day, but both versions can be useful. They can be used for tidying up rough edges for example.

The pointer changes to an arrowhead when it is placed within any marquee, and this indicates that the marquee can be dragged to a different position. As you will soon notice when using Photoshop, the pointer changes to suit the particular tool in use. The arrowhead is the pointer for the Move tool, and Photoshop is indicating an automatic change to this tool when the pointer is within a marquee. If the Control key is operated while dragging a selection, the contents of the marquee are dragged with it. In effect, a cut and paste operation is performed. Note that dragging the marquee thereafter results in the contents moving with it, and there is no need to hold down the Control after the first time.

Another useful ploy is to operate the Spacebar while dragging a marquee onto the screen. This results in the marquee being moved rather than changed in size. Releasing the Spacebar takes things back to the normal sizing mode. It can be difficult to get it right the first time when using the Marquee tool, but the selection is easily "fine tuned" by switching between the sizing and moving modes via the Spacebar.

Multiple selections

Making a new selection while an existing selection is present normally results in the original one being deleted. However, it is possible to have multiple selections. Simply hold down the shift key while making a selection and any existing selection or selections will be left on the screen. One slight snag with this method is that it is not possible to use the Shift

*Fig.3.1 There are four buttons on the Options bar with a Marquee
            tool selected*

key to constrain the Marquee to a square or circle, since it is being used to indicate that a multiple selection is required. With a Marquee tool selected there are four buttons near the left end of the Options bar and some menus to the right (Figure 3.1). As will be explained shortly, one of the menus provides a solution to the problem.

By default the first button (working from left to right) is active, and this sets the selection process to the mode where a new selection replaces any existing ones. Using the next button along sets the mode where multiple selections are possible. With this mode in use it is possible to place several Marquees on the image and still use the Shift key to produce a square or circular selection. Note that in the multiple mode any overlapping selections are merged into a single selection. The selections of Figure 3.2 for example, would be merged into the single selection of Figure 3.3. If necessary, quite complex shapes can be built up in this way.

Subtraction

The third button puts the Marquee tool into Subtraction mode, which enables a "hole" or "knockout" to be placed within an existing selection. In Figure 3.4 an initial large ellipse has been placed at the front of the camera's lens. With the Subtraction mode selected, a smaller ellipse has then been placed within the original ellipse. The Delete key was then operated so that the selected area was erased. This clearly shows

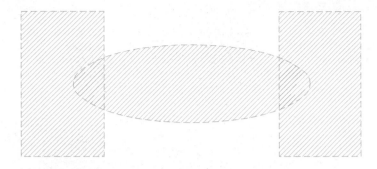

Fig.3.2 These three selections would combine to produce the
selection area shown in Fig.3.3

how the area within the smaller ellipse has been removed from the
selection, since this area has not been erased.

Dragging marquees outside an existing selection is pointless in the
Subtraction mode, since there is no selection to subtract from.
Accordingly, Photoshop will ignore any attempts to do this. Where the
new selection partially overlaps the existing one, the overlapping area
will be removed from the existing selection. This can be useful since it
enables an oversize selection to be nibbled down to exactly the required

Fig.3.3 The combined selection area

*Fig.3.4 It is not necessary to select everything within a selection
outline*

size and shape. With some of the automatic selection methods there is
a tendency to produce small unwanted selection areas, and these are
easily removed using the normal Marquee tool and the subtraction mode.

The final button is the Intersect with Selection button. Normally two
overlapping selections are merged to make one large selection. In the
Intersect mode things operate in the opposite manner, with only the
overlapping sections being used in the combined selection. The two
selections of in the upper section of Figure 3.5 would therefore combine
to produce the much reduced selection in the lower section. This method
can be used to produce selections having shapes that are not otherwise
possible using the basic Marquee tools.

Style

Three options are available from the Style menu on the Options bar
(Figure 3.6). By default the Normal style is selected, and the Marquee
tools then work in the standard fashion described previously. As one

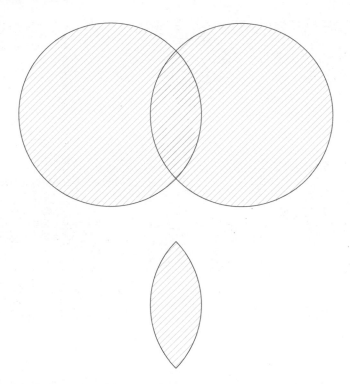

Fig.3.5 The two selections at the top produce the Intersect selection below

would expect, using the Fixed Aspect Ratio mode results in rectangular and elliptical selections having a fixed aspect ratio. This is rather like holding down the Shift key to force a square or circular selection, but other aspect ratios are possible.

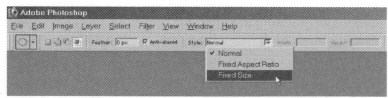

Fig.3.6 The Style menu has three options

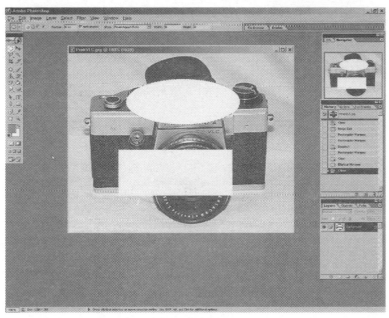

Fig.3.7 Rectangular and eliptical selections

The Width and Height textboxes just to the right of the menu become active when this mode is selected. The default aspect ratio is 1 to 1, but any desired ratio can be entered in the textboxes. In Figure 3.7 a rectangular selection and an elliptical have been added to the screen, and the contents have then been deleted to make the shapes clearly visible. In both cases a width to height ratio of 5 to 2 has been used. Multiple selections are still possible when using a fixed aspect ratio, and the Spacebar can be used to move a selection while it is being created.

This mode overcomes the problem mentioned earlier, where the Spacebar can not be used to constrain the selection to a square or circle, and provide multiple selections. Simply select the Fixed Aspect Ratio mode and make the first selection. Then hold down the Shift key and make further selections. This method is more versatile as aspect ratios other that 1 to 1 are available. Note that it is possible to make a selection, change the aspect ratio, make a further selection, change the ratio again, add another selcotion, and so on.

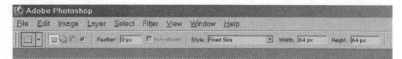

Fig.3.8 Two textboxes on the Options bar permit the width and height of the marquee to be set at fixed amounts

Fixed size

The third option is for a marquee of a fixed size, and the two textboxes are again active when this option is selected (Figure 3.8). They are used to set the width and height of the marquee in pixels. In this mode the marquee is produced by left-clicking the mouse. Dragging the marquee obviously has no effect on its size, but instead moves it around the screen. Consequently, there is no need to hold down the Spacebar in order to move the marquee. Once in position it can be moved in the normal way, and multiple selections are still possible.

Do not press the Delete key in order to clear marquees from the screen. As explained previously, this will delete the selected material, leaving the marquee in place. One or more marquees can be deselected by left-clicking anywhere on the image provided Normal mode is selected and the New Selection button is active. This effectively replaces the current selection with a new one having zero pixels. In the New Selection and Intersect modes it is possible to remove the current selection or selections by left-clicking within one of the selections.

Another method is to right-click on a selection and select Deselect from the popup menu (Figure 3.9). Note that this clears away all the selections if there is more than one, and not just the selection that was right-clicked. The Deselect option is also available from the Select menu on the menu bar. Remember that it is only possible to edit material within a selection when one or more selections are present. In order to edit other areas it is necessary to add another selection to cover the relevant area or delete the existing selections so that the entire image is available for editing. Alternatively, select Inverse from the Select menu so that the selected and non-selected areas are swapped. Use the Inverse option again in order to restore the selections once you have finished editing outside them.

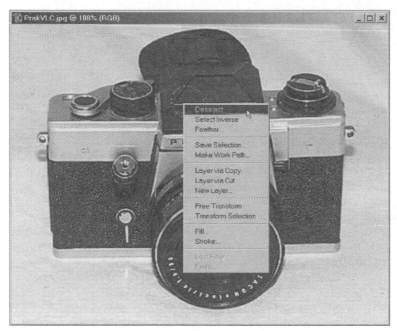

Fig.3.9 A Deselect option is available from the popup menu

Lasso tool

The Marquee tools are adequate for many selection tasks, but they make heavy work or selecting complex shapes. It can be done, but a lot of merging and nibbling is needed to get things right. The Lasso tool is better for selecting awkward shapes since it enables you to draw around the required area. Although it is easy to use in theory, in practice it is difficult to use the Lasso tool with adequate accuracy. Even an experienced and skilled user is unlike to get it right first time. At first it is often a struggle to get anything approximating to the required selection.

A digitising tablet and a stylus is certainly much better than a mouse for this type of thing, and an inexpensive digitising tablet is certainly a worthwhile investment for anyone who uses Photoshop more than occasionally. The merge and subtraction methods work using the Lasso tool, so it is possible to "fine tune" the selection if you do not get it right first time. It is easier to get good accuracy using a zoomed view, so make good use of the pan and zoom facilities when making fine

Fig.3.10 The right-hand piece of leatherette has been selected

adjustments. Most people find that reducing the sensitivity of the mouse or tablet makes it easier to obtain good accuracy. By reducing sensitivity I mean that the pointing device should be set so that more physical movement is required for a given amount of movement on the screen.

To use the Lasso tool you simply drag a line around the area that you wish to select. There is no need to accurately match the start and finish points of the line. Photoshop will automatically connect the start and finish points. On the other hand, leaving a large gap is unlikely to give adequate accuracy. With practice and the inevitable fine adjustments to the marquee, it will usually be possible to obtain the desired result.

In the example of Figure 3.10 the aim was to lighten the leatherette covering on the camera while leaving the rest of the picture unaltered. Work started with the right-hand section, and after a few adjustments the marquee accurately followed the outline of the leatherette, as can just about be seen in Figure 3.10. In Figure 3.11 the selection has been lightened and the rest of the picture is unaffected. It was then just a matter of repeating the process on the left-hand side.

Fig.3.11 Here the selection has been lightened

Polygonal Lasso tool

There are two alternative versions of the Lasso tool available, and the first of them is the Polygonal Lasso tool. This is used to draw irregular polygons, and on the face of it the regular Lasso tool is the more useful. The polygonal version draws straight lines between points drawn on the screen, which means that true curves can not be produced. There is no such limitation with the normal Lasso tool, where freehand drawing can be used to produce any shape, curved or otherwise.

However, as already explained, accurate drawing using the normal Lasso tool is very difficult. Even after you have gained some experience it can be very difficult to get really good accuracy without resorting to a great deal of "fine tuning". Drawing complex shapes by picking points on the outline is very much easier. Although it is not possible to draw true curves, a good approximation can be produced using several short lines. In practice, selections made using the Polygonal Lasso tool are often sufficiently accurate without the need for fine adjustments, which is rarely if ever true when using the normal Lasso tool.

Fig.3.12 The piece of leatherette on the left has been selected using the Polygonal Lasso tool

In Figure 3.12 the left-hand piece of leatherette has been selected using the Polygonal Lasso tool, and no "fine tuning" has been applied to the initial selection. The lightening has been applied in Figure 3.13. The increase in brightness has been deliberately overdone in both Figure 3.11 and Figure 3.13 to make the outline of the selection more obvious. The left-hand selection, made without any editing, is at least as accurate as the right-hand section, which required a substantial amount of adjustment. As always with this type of thing, it is a matter of using whichever tool you find to be the best for the job. In most cases it will almost certainly be the Polygonal Lasso tool rather than the standard version.

Using the Polygonal Lasso tool is very straightforward. Start by left-clicking to place the first point on the outline. The program then draws a line from this first point to the current position of the pointer, making it easy to position the next point on the outline. The next point is produced by left-clicking again, and the "rubber band" line then appears from the second point to the current position of the pointer. Add all the points needed to complete the outline and then left-click again on the first point

Fig.3.13 The leatherette on the left has been lightened

to close the outline. The final point must be placed quite accurately, and a small circle appears on the pointer when it is close enough to close the shape (Figure 3.14). An alternative method of closing the shape is to double-click on the final point. Photoshop will then automatically place the line from there to the starting point. The final point was too

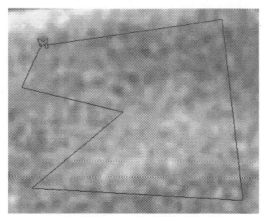

Fig.3.14 A circle appears on the pointer when it is close enough to the starting point to close the selection

Fig.3.15 This time the leatherette on the left has been selected using the Magnetic Lasso tool

close to the first point if the selection disappears when the mouse is double clicked. The two clicks close and then deselect the selection. Going back one stage using the Undo facility or the History palette will restore the selection.

If, having just placed a point, you decide that it is not positioned accurately, operate the Delete key to erase it so that another attempt can be made. In fact the Delete key can be used repeatedly to go on deleting points right back to the first one. This ability to change your mind and retrace your steps is a huge advantage over the standard Lasso tool, where once you have started you have to go on until you have finished. Of course, using the Delete key once the shape has been closed will erase everything within the selection, as normal. Any changes to the last few points must therefore be made before the selection is closed. Provided the shape has not been closed, operating the Escape key will completely remove all the lines.

Fig.3.16 The leatherette has been lightened, and the selection has proved to be quite accurate

Magnetic Lasso tool

This is a sort of semi-automatic version of the standard Lasso tool. As already pointed out, getting accurate results using the normal Lasso tool is quite tricky. Photoshop will faithfully reproduce every little error in your rendering of the outline, and some editing will usually be required once the outline has been completed. The Magnetic Lasso tool makes life much easier by looking for an outline to follow rather than simply following the exact path of the pointer. How well or otherwise this works depends on how well an object's outline is defined. It should work very well if there is plenty of contrast in shade or colour. If there is no outline to follow, the Magnetic Lasso is not the tool for the job. It is probably not the best tool for the job if there is only an indistinct or intermittent outline to follow.

In Figure 3.15 I have undone the original processing on the left side of the image and used the Magnetic Lasso tool to select the leatherette again. The outline was drawn using a mouse and I was not especially

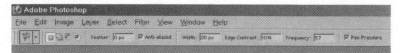

Fig.3.17 The adjustments available via the Options bar enable the Magnetic Lasso tool to be set for optimum results

careful when following the outline. Nevertheless, the Magnetic Lasso tool has done quite a good job of following the outline of the leatherette. It has not gone right into the very sharp corners, but in other respects it has performed very well. In Figure 3.16 the increase in brightness has been added, and this shows the outline of the selection more clearly. There are still no major errors in evidence and this method of selection has proved to be quick and accurate on this occasion.

There are some parameters in the Options bar (Figure 3.17) that enable the Magnetic Lasso tool to be optimised for a given situation. The Width (detection width) setting controls how close the pointer has to be to an edge for the Magnetic Lasso tool to latch onto it. The larger this figure the less accurately you have to follow the outline. Do not be tempted to use a large figure for this setting though. The line might tend to jump off its intended path and onto another outline, particularly if the pointer is allowed to stray well away from the correct path. The Width setting is in pixels incidentally.

Edge Contrast

The Edge Contrast figure determines the difference in brightness value required for an outline to be recognised. Using a low value enables the outline to be followed even when there is relatively little contrast between the object and the background. Unfortunately, it also increases the likelihood of the line jumping over to a different outline or jumping to any small areas of slight contrast. A small Edge Contrast value normally has to be accompanied by a small Width value and careful drawing of the selection outline. This tool works best with well defined objects and a reasonably high Edge Contrast value.

The Frequency setting controls the number of anchor points that will be added as the outline is drawn. These anchor points are shown as tiny squares on the line while it is being drawn. The higher the number, the more anchor points that are used and the more accurately intricate outlines can be tracked. In the leatherette example used previously, the

FakeLeica.jpg @ 100% (RGB)

*Fig.3.18 The leatherette on the right has been selected using the
         Magic Wand tool*

outline did not go right into the sharp corners. A high value gives better
accuracy with this type of thing, but note that the maximum permissible
value is 100. On the down side, a high value might have a tendency to
produce rough edges, particularly when used with a low Edge Contrast
value.

Using the Magic Lasso tool is again very straightforward. Drag the line
making sure that the pointer is kept quite close to the outline you are
trying to follow. Release the left mouse button when the pointer is back
at the starting point. Alternatively, double click the mouse with the pointer
close to the starting point. Photoshop will then draw a line between the
final and starting points, tracking what it considers to be the correct path.

If things go badly wrong, operate the Escape key to completely remove
the line so that you can start from scratch. The last anchor point added
can be removed by operating the delete key, and this key can be operated
repeatedly to remove further anchor points back down the line. Keep
the pointer still while deleting anchor points so that no new ones are
added while you are trying to remove some of the existing points. This

Fig.3.19 The Magic Wand tool has found the outline accurately

tool often gives better results with the pointer kept just to one side of the required path rather than trying to track the pointer right over the path.

Magic Wand tool

With the Magic Wand tool there is no need to draw around the object you wish to select. You just left-click at a suitable point on the image and Photoshop automatically selects the right area. Of course, in reality it is not quite as simple as that, and Photoshop might not get it right. The Magic Wand tool tries to find an outline based on the colour values of the pixels. If there is good colour contrast between the object you are trying to select and the background it is likely that the Magic Wand tool will do a good job. Results are less sure if the object blends into the background at some points.

Figure 3.18 shows the original version of the fake Leica photograph, with the leatherette on the right-hand side selected using the Magic Wand tool. The tool was left-clicked on the leatherette, just inside its upper limit. To give this method a realistic chance of success it is usually

Fig.3.20 When used on the right-hand side the Magic Wand tool has found a few islands

essential to click the tool close to the edge of the object you are trying to select. In this case there is excellent colour contrast between the black leatherette and the silver of the metalwork, and the outline has been found with a high degree of accuracy.

There is an apparent flaw, in that a blemish in the leatherette has been outlined as well. When the Magic Wand tool produces islands such as this, even though they are totally within the main selection, they do not form part of the selection. The blemish is therefore not selected, and it will not be processed along with the rest of the leatherette. This is demonstrated by Figure 3.19 where the increase in brightness has been applied and the leatherette has been deselected so that the final result can be seen more clearly.

A massive increase in brightness has not caused the lighter parts in the blemish to go "whiter than white" because they were not selected. This might be what is needed, or it might not. In this case it probably gives better results than having the entire area selected. Where necessary, areas that evade the Magic Wand tool can be added to the selection using a Marquee tool in the Add to Selection mode. Using this method

Fig.3.21 The increase in brightness has gone according to plan

it is possible to add areas outside the selection, or areas can be removed using the subtract mode. The four mode buttons are available with all selection tools, and permit these tools and modes to be freely mixed.

Islands

It is only fair to point out that the Magic Wand tool does not always work this well, but on this occasion it has found the required outline with total precision, and it took just one mouse click. In Figure 3.20 the Magic Wand tool has been used on the left-hand piece of leatherette, and it has again found the outline quite accurately. It has also found several outlines within the main selection, but once again this is of no practical consequence. One of these goes around the flash socket, and there is no problem here. This is not part of the leatherette and should not be included. As pointed out previously, this type of thing is easily added to the selection where necessary. For the sake of this example we will assume that this needs to be left at the current brightness setting, and it will be left out of the selection.

Figure 3.21 shows the effect of increasing the brightness, and things have gone more or less according to plan. The socket has been left with

its original brightness level, and the outline of the leatherette has been found quite accurately. There is a tiny patch that has been missed at the top, and another one just to the right of this. One way of correcting this type of thing is to use the Magic Wand tool to select the omitted areas and then make the necessary adjustments. This has been done in Figure 3.22, which

Fig.3.22 Imperfections have been corrected

shows the relevant section of the photograph. It is often easier to use retouching techniques to correct this type of problem, and it is a matter of using whichever method you find the most convenient.

Settings

There are a few Magic Wand settings available from the Options bar. The Tolerance setting is important, and it is unlikely that good results will be obtained unless this is adjusted to suit each task. It controls the amount of colour contrast that is needed for Photoshop to perceive the change as an edge. In Figure 3.23 a fairly high setting of 40 has been used, and the outlines have been found quite accurately for both pieces of leatherette. There are one or two other areas that have been selected within the main selection, but as we have already seen, these are of no real consequence. They could be added to the selection quite easily.

A much lower setting of 10 has been used in Figure 3.24, and only two very small areas have been selected. The higher sensitivity has resulted in the pattern of the leatherette being detected and used as the outline. As this demonstration clearly shows, unless the tolerance value is in the right "ball park" there is no chance of the Magic Wand tool finding the

Fig.3.23 A Tolerance setting of 40 has provided good results

Fig.3.24 Little has been selected with the Tolerance set at 10

Fig.3.25 All the dark pixels have been selected with the Contiguous option switched off

right outline. Be prepared to experiment with various values in an attempt to find one that accurately locates the outline.

It is also worth trying various points near and on the outline when left-clicking the Magic Wand tool. Bear in mind that the Magic Wand tool is colour conscious, and it is an outline of a certain colour that it seeks, not simply a path of about the same brightness. It therefore works best with objects that are predominantly the same colour, such as a patch of blue sky.

Contiguous

By default the Contiguous checkbox is ticked, which means that a continuous path of pixels is sought by the program, which tries to find an outline. It will also find any "islands" within the outline and automatically subtract them from the selection. The Magic Wand tool simply selects any pixels at colours within its tolerance setting when this checkbox is not ticked. In other words, it tries to find any pixels of the right colour range, anywhere on the image, and it does not try to find outlines.

Fig.3.26 This shows more clearly the pixels that were selected

This is demonstrated in Figure 3.25, where the Magic Wand has been left-clicked on a dark area of the leatherette. Anything black, anywhere on the image, has been selected. This is made clearer in Figure 3.26, where the selection has been deleted. Both pieces of leatherette have disappeared, along with the dark area at the front of the lens, the shadow under the lens, and numerous other dark areas. The non-contiguous mode will often select far too much. However, if it accurately finds the area you wish to select, it could still be a good choice. Remember that the subtraction mode can be used to remove the unwanted selections. The unwanted selections can soon be mopped up with the Rectangular Marquee or Lasso tool.

Anti-aliased

The Anti-aliased checkbox is also ticked by default. This is also available and used by default with the Lasso tools. Anti-aliasing smoothes the edges of the selection or selections, which often gives better results than having it faithfully follow every nook and cranny in an outline. On the other hand, anti-aliasing will probably give less satisfactory results if the required selection genuinely has rough edges. The smoothing will cause parts of the required area to be omitted and (or) material outside the required area to be included. With an area that has a smooth and well defined outline it is unlikely to make much difference one way or the other. Once again, it is a matter of experimenting to find the mode that gives the best results.

Select menu

Do not overlook the facilities available from the Select menu (Figure 3.27). A similar menu is also available by right-clicking within a selection. A Feather option is available when some selection tools are selected, and it also appears in the Options bar when appropriate. It is primarily intended for use with cut/copy and paste operations. There can be problems with objects that pasted into an image having a two dimensional cardboard cut-out appearance.

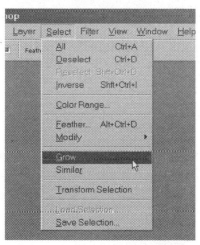

Feathering offers one approach to integrating a pasted object into an image without getting the cardboard cut-out effect. It gives a blurred edge that blends into the new image more realistically, and the width of the feathering (in pixels) can be specified on the Options bar prior to selection. A small dialogue box appears when

Fig.3.27 The Select menu offers some useful facilities

Feathering is chosen from the Select menu, and this is used to specify a value for the pixel width. This method can be used to add feathering to an existing selection.

Figure 3.28 shows the fake Leica camera copied from the original image and pasted onto a plain background. The outline has not been traced very accurately, and the image is therefore a bit rough at the edges. Figure 3.29 shows the original image with the Feather setting at 50 pixels,

*Fig.3.28 The camera has been pasted onto a plain background, and
the outline is clearly a bit approximate in places*

and the outline has become very approximate indeed. The setting has
been deliberately set high so that the effect of feathering is shown very
clearly. Note how the selection line cuts through the wind-on knob at the
top left-hand side and the leatherette in the bottom right-hand corner.

In Figure 3.30 the camera has again been copied and then pasted onto
a plain background, but the effect is now very different. What was
previously a clearly defined edge has become extremely blurred. The
central part of the image is sharp, as in the original pasted version. Moving
out towards the edge, the image is a combination of the pasted material
and the background. The pasted image becomes progressively weaker
towards the outer limit. Feathering helps to smooth edges and give
more natural looking results when used in small amounts. When used
more heavily it can give quite a good soft focus effect, as in this example

Modify submenu

There are four options available in the Modify submenu. The border
option produces a small dialogue box that requests a pixel value to be
entered. Instead of selecting the area within an outline, a band of pixels
centred on the outline is selected. The value entered controls the width

Fig.3.29 A Feathering value of 50 gives very approximate results

Fig.3.30 The feathering has produced a form of soft-focus effect

Fig.3.31 The original selections made using the Magic Wand tool

of the band. The Smooth option does precisely that, and it will smooth out jagged edges in the marquee. The Expand and Contract options simply enlarge or shrink the selection by the specified number of pixels.

One application of the last two options is to take slightly more of an image than is really required for a copy and paste operation. The pasted background is then painted over using the existing background of the destination image. This is not a quick way of doing things, but it ensures that all the required source material is copied with no little bits missing, and the pasted image should integrate quite well with the rest of the destination image. You may find that some selection methods tend to outline slightly too much or too little material. The Expand and Contract options provide quick and easy solutions to these problems.

Grow

The Grow option in the main Select menu should not be confused with the Expand option in the Modify submenu. Grow does not expand the border of the selection by a certain number of pixels. Instead, it looks for

Fig.3.32 The enlarged selections are very accurate

pixels of a similar colour around the border, and the selection then grows into these. In Figure 3.31 the Magic Wand tool has been used to select the two pieces of leatherette, and it has again done quite a good job. However, there are a few "islands" and a few pixels have been omitted near the edges.

Using the Grow facility has enlarged the selection slightly (Figure 3.32), engulfing a number of pixels that escaped previously. In fact the selection matches the leatherette outlines so accurately that it is hard to see the marquees in Figure 3.32. Deleting the selections (Figure 3.33) shows how few pixels have escaped. The selection is remarkably accurate for one that was produced using fully automatic methods. It is possible to use the grow facility repeatedly in an attempt to encompass every last pixel, but doing so is likely to enlarge the selection too far in some areas. It is generally better to manually select any awkward pixels. Where a selection process has missed some pixels at the edges, the Grow facility will usually yield more accurate results than the Expand facility.

Fig.3.33 Deleting the selections shows how accurate they were

Similar

The Similar function in the Select menu looks for pixels of similar colour to the existing selection and adds them to the selection. Note that pixels anywhere on the image will be included if they provide a suitable colour match. This is demonstrated by Figure 3.34 where a black area of the image was selected initially. With the aid of the Similar function, all the black pixels were then selected and deleted. Clearly, all the black or very dark pixels were added to the selection when the Similar option was used. This is similar to using the Magic Wand tool with the Contiguous option switched off.

Inverse

The Inverse option simply deselects everything that is currently selected, and selects everything that was not previously selected. In Figure 3.35 the two pieces of leatherette have again been selected, the Inverse option has been used, and then the Delete button has been operated. This has resulted in everything but the leatherette being erased. When it is

Fig.3.34 The Similar function has found all the dark pixels, which have been deleted

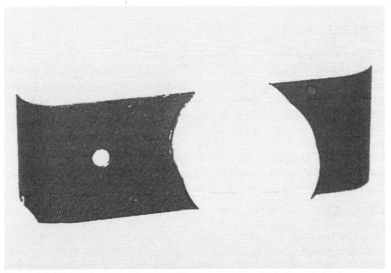

Fig.3.35 The Inverse option enables everything but the original selection to be processed

Fig.3.36 The background has been deleted

necessary to select a large percentage of an image it is often easier to select the other bits and then use the Inverse option.

This technique is used a great deal to remove the existing background from an object so that a new one can be added. In Figure 3.36 the camera has been selected, the Inverse command has been used, and the area outside the camera has been deleted. Sometimes this is all that is needed, but in most cases a new background is added. With a complex background the object can be copied and pasted onto the background image. With a simple coloured or graduated background it is just a matter of "pouring" it into place using the Paint Bucket or Gradient tool. The Inverse selection must be left in place so that the new background flows around the object.

In Figure 3.37 the Gradient tool has been used to provide the new background. This is a rather spectacular blue that loses something in the translation to a grey scale, but it gives an idea of the type of thing that can be achieved. There will usually be one or two rough edges on the object, but normal retouching techniques can be used to smooth these

Fig.3.37 A more dynamic background has bee added using the Gradient tool

out and give a better appearance. It is worth trying this technique with a few images even if you have no immediate need for it. Any errors in the selection show up like the proverbial sore thumb once the background is removed, so it is a good way of perfecting your selection skills.

Finally

It would be an exaggeration to say that every image will require selective processing. No processing at all will be needed if the source image is very good, and processing the entire image should be sufficient if there is just a minor problem with the overall colour balance, brightness, or something of this type. In many cases though, you will need to process some parts of the image while leaving others untouched. If you wish to get creative and use bits of images to enhance other images, some fairly skilful selection will have to be used.

Unfortunately, real-world images do not usually have nice clearly defined edges that consist of a few long straight lines. They tend to be complex

Fig.3.38 The only blues in this photograph are in the sky

and knobbly, with a tendency to merge into the background in places. It is only on rare occasions that a single click of the Magic Wand tool will be sufficient to make precisely the required selection. Try experimenting with some images to find the best ways of handling various situations.

Use the Lasso and Magic Wand tools with various settings to familiarise yourself with their effects on results. Get used to the Subtraction, Addition, and Intersect modes, which will normally be needed to "fine tune" the initial selection. Do not forget the facilities available from the Select menu as these can often save a great deal of time.   In order to fully utilize Photoshop's abilities it is important to get to grips with the selection facilities, so be prepared to put some effort into learning the techniques involved.

The obvious way of making selections is to start drawing the outlines using the Lasso tools, perhaps trying the Magic Wand tool first in the hope that it will automatically find the correct outline for each area that you indicate. It pays to remember that you can select pixels of a similar colour using the Similar option in the Select menu or the Magic Wand

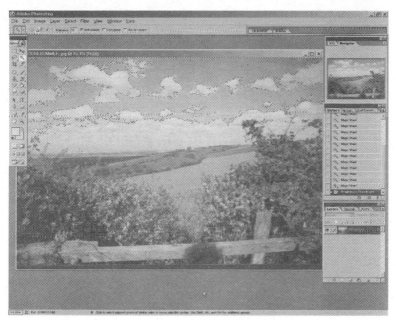

Fig.3.39 The blue areas of sky have been selected and darkened

tool in the Contiguous option switched off. The Magic Wand tool set for non-contiguous operation is very good at selecting things like all the areas of blue sky.

Suppose that the blue areas of sky in the photograph of Figure 3.38 had to be made bluer and darker to give a more dramatic sky. You will have to take my word about the colours, but the fields and hedges are a mixture of bright yellow and various greens. There are browns in the wooden fence, various greys in the clouds and castle ruins in the distance, and some pink blossom in the foreground. The only blue is in the blue areas of cloud-free sky.

One approach would be to use the Magic Wand tool in the non-contiguous mode and a fairly high tolerance setting. On the face of it, with no other blue areas in the photograph it would only pick out the blue sky. In practice some of the pale grey areas would almost certainly be included together with blue sky. Some experimentation with the tolerance setting might give the desired result, but it is often better to use a low setting and left-click on areas of light, mid, and dark blue. Using the Addition mode, the required areas can be picked out quite accurately with a few mouse clicks. In Figure 3.39 the required areas have been selected using this method and the blue sky has been altered (although this might not show up well in black and white reproduction).

Even if this approach does make a few unwanted selections, these will probably be easy to remove using one of the Marquee tools in the subtraction mode. It is certainly worth trying in situations where numerous areas of approximately the same colour must be selected. With any method, if results do not look quite right try going back to the selection, add a small amount of feathering, and apply the processing again. This should avoid having an obvious edge on the processed material. Bear in mind that the non-contiguous mode is colour conscious, and that it is not similar levels of brightness that it seeks. Using this mode with a greyscale image will probably result in everything being selected!

Points to remember

Selective processing opens up a wide range of creative possibilities in addition to permitting better editing of images. However, accurately selecting the required material can be a tricky and time consuming business.

Photoshop has a range of selection tools that make the selection process as quick and easy as possible. You can simply draw the selection outline onto the screen using the Lasso tool, but it is often quicker and more accurate to use the Magnetic Lasso and Magic Wand tools.

The Magic Wand tool will select all the pixels in a certain colour range when the tick is removed from the Contiguous checkbox. This is useful for selecting blue sky, the petals of flowers, or anything where the required material is predominantly one colour.

Using the four buttons on the Options bar it is possible to build up selections piece by piece, and to nibble away at the selection. It is also possible to switch from one selection tool to another while doing this. An initial selection can be made using (say) the Magic Wand tool, and then it can be "fine tuned" using the Lasso and Marquee tools.

Various settings are available on the Options bar when using the Magnetic Lasso and Magic Wand tools. These automatic and semi-automatic selection tools will only work well if the image provides adequate contrasts, and suitable settings are used on the Options bar.

Do not forget the facilities that are available from the Select menu. The Grow option is very useful if the Magnetic Lasso or Magic Wand tool has selected slightly less than an entire object. The Inverse option swaps the selected and non-selected areas. Sometimes the easiest way of doing things is to select the area that you do not wish to change and then use the Inverse option.

The Copy and Paste facilities can be used to copy selected objects from one image to another. It can be difficult to get really convincing results, but this technique has tremendous creative possibilities.

As with most parts of Photoshop, it is a matter of "practice makes perfect". Making accurate selections can be difficult at first, but once you have gained some experience it will usually be possible to get the desired result reasonably quickly.

Selections and paths

Copy and Paste

Having learnt to how select the right parts of the image you are ready to move on to processing the image. It is not always necessary to select part of the image before undertaking some form of processing, and things like colour and contrast adjustments are often applied to the entire image. If this processing leaves some areas that are less than perfect it is time to try some selective processing. The actual processing is the same whether it is applied globally or selectively. If you select an area or several areas and then apply some form of processing, it will only be applied to the selected part or parts of the image. The available processes are exactly the same for global and selective processing, and they are applied in exactly the same way. This makes it much easier to learn and use Photoshop.

With nothing selected, some forms of processing will automatically be applied to the entire picture. Changes to brightness and contrast for example, fall into this category. A few types of processing require a selection to be made first, and they simply have no effect unless something is selected. The Delete key for example, will only delete selections. Of course, where necessary the standard Select All facility can be used to select a complete image. Note though, that there is no Select All option in the Edit menu. Instead, the All option must be selected from the Select menu.

The usual Cut, Copy, and Paste facilities are available from the Edit menu. If the Cut facility is used, a "hole" will be left in the image where the selected material used to be, and it will be filled with the background colour, as in Figure 4.1 where a tree has been removed from the image. The background is white by default, as in this example. A common application of the cut and paste technique is to move an object to a new

Fig.4.1   The tree on the right has been cut from the image

position in the image, but the "hole" left at the original position has to be healed using one of the Clone tools. These techniques are covered in chapter 7 and this aspect of things will not be considered here.

The tree has been "transplanted" in Figure 4.2 and the gap it left has been retouched using the Clone tool. The tree was removed using the Cut command, pasted back onto the image, and then repositioned to the right using the Move tool. Finally, the gap left by the Cut operation was retouched. The same result could be obtained using the Copy and Paste commands, with the original tree then being retouched. However, most people find it easier to paint the background into the vacant space left by a Cut command, rather than painting over the unwanted original material. I suppose that it should not be more difficult to cover the original material, but in practice most people find this method more confusing. Presumably it is more natural to fill a void than it is to paint over valid material.

Material can be pasted from one picture to another, and provided there is sufficient memory available it is possible to have both pictures loaded

Fig.4.2 The tree has been pasted further to the right, and the hole it left behind has been retouched

into Photoshop so that you can cut/copy and paste straight from one image to the other. Remember left-click on the title bar of the second image to make it the current one, prior to pasting the new material onto the image. It will otherwise be pasted back onto the source image.

Layers

Paste operations can be a bit confusing for newcomers to Photoshop as the pasted material is automatically placed onto a new layer. New layers are generated by some other facilities of Photoshop. For example, each piece of text that is added is automatically placed onto its own layer. Without realising it, you can soon have quite a large number of layers that Photoshop has generated. As a consequence of this, you find that most of the image can not be edited, or so it appears anyway.

The point of using one layer per element in the image is that it makes it easy to edit each element separately. For example, text or pasted material can be moved by selecting the correct layer and then dragging it using the Move tool. There is no need to bother about selecting the material that must be moved, since there is nothing else on that layer. Move the entire layer and you move the required elements in the image. There is no need to heal gaps left when the material is moved, because it does not leave any.

Think of layers in terms of each one being on a separate piece of transparent film, with the pieces of film laid one on top of the other. Material on a piece of film near the top of the pile will obscure some of the material on lower layers. If the layer is moved to one side, the obscured material can be seen, but a different part of the image is obscured on the lower layers. Hence objects can be moved around without the need to fill in any gaps left by the changes. If an object is cut from an image it will still leave a "hole", but once it is pasted onto a new layer it can be moved around without damaging the underlying image.

Automatically generated layers can give beginners problems because the new layer becomes the current one, and it is not possible to edit anything on another layer. Attempts to do so either have no effect or produce error messages. Normally it is only possible to edit the current layer.

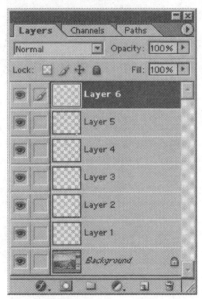

Fig.4.3 All the layers are listed in the Layers palette

Layers are covered elsewhere in this book, as the need arises, but a few essentials will be explained here. The Layers palette has a list of all the layers in the image, and initially there is just one that is called Background. Any layers that are added by text or paste operations are added above any existing layers, and they are called Layer 1, Layer 2, Layer 3, and so on (Figure 4.3). The position of a layer in the list is the same as its position in the image. For example, Layer 2 is on top of Layer 1 and the Background layer, and anything on Layer 2 therefore covers these lower layers. Similarly, anything on Layer 3 would obstruct the view of Layer 2 and the lower layers.

It is possible to move a layer to a new position in the list and the image by dragging its name in the list to a new position. In Figure 4.4 this has been done with Layer 5, which has been moved two positions lower in the layer hierarchy. Note that the layers are not automatically renamed, and Layer 5 retains that name even though it is only three positions above the Background layer. It is the position in the list that counts, and not the names. As pointed out previously, it is only possible to edit the current layer. It is merely necessary to left-click on a layer's name in the list in order to make it the current layer and editable. There are eye icons in the left-hand column of the list. Left-clicking on an eye icon makes the relevant layer invisible,

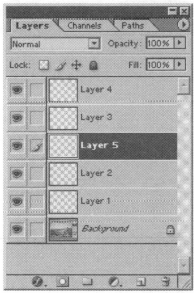

Fig.4.4 Layers can be dragged to new positions

and left-clicking again makes it reappear. It is often necessary to switch off upper layers so that lower ones can be seen properly for editing purposes.

Cropping

I would guess that cropping is the Photoshop function that I use most frequently, and it is certainly one that most users will resort to quite often. It can be used to slightly alter the composition of a picture, removing unwanted material near the edge. Group shots in public places for example, often have half a bystander encroaching at one side of the picture. Perhaps a scan has gone slightly wrong, resulting in a blank strip along one or more edges of the picture where slightly too much has been scanned.

Many cameras give slightly more on the film than was included in the viewfinder. This "tunnel vision" is apparently used to compensate for the fact that machine prints cover slightly less than the full negative or transparency. However, most film scanners do cover the full frame, and

Fig.4.5 The areas that will be cropped are darkened

therefore give more than was included in the viewfinder. Most digital cameras also have less coverage in the viewfinder than appears in the image, but the reason for this is less than obvious. Anyway, an excess of coverage, for whatever reason, is easily corrected using Photoshop.

Image quality

It is possible to drastically alter the composition by massively cropping an image. With many photographs, but particularly with very wide-angle shots, there are often many good pictures within the overall scene. Many of the photographs used in magazines and newspapers have been cropped from much larger images. Bear in mind that the maximum usable print size is reduced proportionately if an image is cropped. The higher the quality of the original image, the greater the scope you have for using creative cropping.

With a top quality negative and a good film scanner it might be possible to obtain an image having 10 million or more pixels and the image quality to match. This might also be possible using a flatbed scanner and a top

Fig.4.6 The cropped version of the picture

quality print. Using a third of the image area it should still be possible to produce a reasonable A4 size print. A digital camera having 3 million or so pixels can just about produce an A4 print from the full-frame image, so cropping the image down to about 1 million pixels will limit the print to about postcard size. Creative cropping requires a very high quality source or you have to settle for small print sizes.

The Toolbox includes a cropping tool that can be used to crop a rectangular area. In Figure 4.5 it has been used to crop the black strip along the bottom of the picture that was caused by scanning a slightly excessive area. The sides of the picture have also been cropped slightly. It is easy to see which parts of the picture will be cropped, as these are shown much darker than the rest of the picture. Eight handles appear on the outline of the cropped area, and these can be dragged to adjust the size of the selection. The selection can be dragged to a new position by using any part of it other than the handles.

Press the Return key to actually go ahead and crop the picture (Figure 4.6), or right-clicking anywhere on the image and selecting crop from the popup has the same effect. A third option is to select Crop from the

Fig.4.7 This elliptical crop has not produced the desired result

Image menu. Right-click and select Cancel to remove the selection, or press the Escape key. It is also possible to crop an image by selecting an area using the standard version of the Marquee tool and then choosing Crop from the Image menu.

On the face of it, the image can be cropped to a non-rectangular shape by using one of the Marquee tools or the Magic Wand tool and then selecting Crop from the Image menu. In practice this method will not provide the desired result. An elliptical selection has been made in Figure 4.7 and then the Crop function has been used. The picture is still rectangular, and it is just large enough to accommodate the selection.

The problem is that the image must be rectangular as this is all that most image file formats support. The desired effect can still be obtained by first cropping the image, as before, to remove most of the unwanted material. Then select the Inverse option from the Select menu so that everything outside the ellipse is selected. Pressing the Delete key then clears everything outside the ellipse, leaving what is effectively an elliptical picture. Figure 4.8 shows the end result, which will work just as well with much more elaborate shapes; including text produced using the Type Mask tools.

Fig.4.8 Some further processing has deleted the material outside the ellipse

Correcting perspective

The Crop tool can also be used to correct problems with perspective, such as converging verticals. This problem mainly occurs when buildings are photographed at relatively short range. The camera is usually aimed upwards slightly in order to get the top of the building into the photograph and avoid an excessive amount of empty foreground. Unfortunately, doing things this way results in the sides of the buildings leaning inwards towards the top. This is caused by a normal perspective effect, with the tops of the buildings looking smaller because they are further away. It is an effect that is mainly associated with wide-angle lenses. It tends to be more noticeable with wide-angle lenses as they give exaggerated perspective, but converging verticals are produced whenever the camera is used with a slight upward tilt.

While converging horizontals give an acceptable perspective effect, converging verticals tend to be perceived as the buildings being tilted away from the viewer and falling over. Large format cameras have movements that can be used to avoid converging verticals, and there are expensive perspective control lenses available for some 35 millimetre

Fig.4.9 This photograph has pronounced converging verticals

and medium format cameras. Using Photoshop you can take the photograph complete with converging verticals and correct it later.

The photograph of Figure 4.9 of a well known statue and clock tower shows strong converging verticals. Big Ben is slanting away from the left side of the photograph and the plinth of the statue shows a similar problem on the other side. Of course, you might be quite happy with this type of thing, as it can produce some dynamic results, but it is easily removed using the Crop tool if it is not what is required. Start by selecting the entire image using the Crop tool, and then tick the Perspective checkbox on the Options bar.

There will be the usual eight handles on the outline of the selection, but they operate in a different manner with the Perspective option activated. Normally, moving one of the handles in a corner results in the selection box increasing or decreasing in size, but the aspect ratio remains unchanged. The handles in the corners can be freely moved around when the Perspective option selected. To correct converging verticals the top left-hand handle is moved to the right, so that the left side of the selection box is parallel to the converging vertical on that side of the image. The top right-hand handle is moved to the left, so that·the right side of the selection box is parallel to the converging vertical on that side of the image. This gives something like Figure 4.10.

Fig.4.10 The upper corner handles have been moved inwards

Fig.4.11 The cropped picture has much "straighter" verticals

Next the cropping is applied by pressing the return key, selecting Crop from the Image menu, or double clicking within the selection box. The areas outside the selection box are then cropped, and the image is stretched back into a rectangle. In doing so, the converging verticals are straightened, as in Figure 4.11. In practice it might take a few attempts to get the desired effect. It should be possible though, provided the image does not have any strong curvature near the edges. Curvature can be a problem with some older wide-angle lenses and very wide-angle zoom lenses. If necessary, you just have to settle for the best compromise.

Rotation

In the Image menu there are four rotation options in the Rotate Canvas submenu (Figure 4.12). The first three of these rotate the image 90 degrees clockwise or counter-clockwise, and by 180 degrees. Sometimes the image from a digital camera or scanner will need one of these options in order to produce an image that has the correct orientation. The fourth option enables the image to be rotated by an arbitrary amount. In other words, you can specify the degree of rotation and the direction. The small window of Figure 4.13 appears when the Arbitrary option is selected. Note that you are not restricted to an integer value,

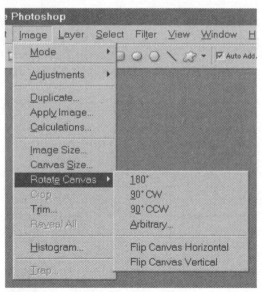

Fig.4.12 Four rotation options are available

and rotation by (say) 2.5 degrees is permissible. It is therefore possible to rotate the image with a high degree of precision, provided it has suitably high resolution.

Arbitrary rotation can be used creatively, but its main use is to correct sloping horizons and similar image faults. The photograph of Figure 4.14 has a very pronounced sloping horizon, which is made all the more obvious because the horizon is

Fig.4.13 A precise amount of rotation can be entered

very near the top of the picture. I am very proficient at producing wonky horizons, but in this case I have the excuse that the photograph was taken leaning out from a bridge. Some of the bridge is just visible down the left edge of the photograph. Sloping horizons and interiors that are keeling over apparently rank as two of the most common faults in photographs.

Fig.4.14 This picture has a severe case of sloping horizon syndrome

Fig.4.15 The picture has been rotated, but more work is needed

To correct this type of fault the appropriate radio button must be operated so that the image is rotated in the right direction, and you have to guess the correct amount of rotation. Initially there is a tendency to overestimate the amount of rotation required. In most cases only about one degree or so is needed, but in this case the error is larger than normal. I tried three degrees initially, but gradually increased this to 4.1 degrees. Placing a guide on the horizon (Figure 4.15) makes it easy to judge whether or not it is horizontal. It is usually necessary to undo the rotation and try again a few times, but it should not take long to get it right.

As can be seen from Figure 4.16, Photoshop automatically increases the size of the canvas so that is fully accommodates the rotated image. This leaves four blank areas that must be cropped or retouched. Cropping is quicker and easier, but some content near the edges of the frame will be lost. In the final version of Figure 4.16 a mixture of the two has been used. Also, the canvas has been increased in size slightly at the top, and some more sky has been added. The final image might not be perfect, but it is certainly a lot more acceptable than the original. Most collections of snapshots have a number of pictures that can be rescued using little more than a degree or so or rotation.

Fig.4.16 The final version of the photograph, complete with a "straight" horizon

Quick method

There is a much quicker and easier method available if the image is to be cropped, and there is no need to retain as much as the original image as possible. Start by dragging a large selection onto the screen using the Crop tool, but it is essential to leave some unselected areas around the selection so that you have room to manoeuvre. Then drag on the image but outside the selected area. This rotates the selection, and it must be carefully rotated so that the top edge is parallel to the horizon. Next, make any necessary adjustments to the selection by dragging the handles in the usual way.

Fig.4.17 Using the Crop tool to provide rotation

This should produce something like Figure 4.17, and Figure 4.18 shows the cropped version of the image. As before, the horizon has been straightened and a much more acceptable image has been produced. With a horizon that is seriously askew it is necessary to crop a significant amount of material from the edges of the picture. However, this method provides an almost instant fix where such cropping is acceptable.

Flipping

There are two extra options in the Rotate Image submenu (Figure 4.19), and these permit the image to be flipped horizontally or vertically. The Flip Canvas Horizontal option is mainly used where it is felt that a reversal of the image will give a composition that will fit better into a page layout. It works well with something like a still-life photograph where there is nothing to give away the fact that the image has been reversed. Figures 4.20 and 4.21 show "before" and "after" versions of a photograph that has been flipped horizontally.

Fig.4.18 The cropped and rotated image

It is essential to take due care when using the flip facility as it is easy to "drop a clanger". With most photographs it will be pretty obvious if they are flipped horizontally. Any text for example, will be converted into

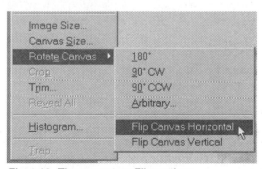

Fig.4.19 There are two Flip options

Fig.4.20 The original version of the photograph

Fig.4.21 This version has been flipped horizontally

Fig.4.22 Can you spot the deliberate mistake?

"mirror" writing in the flipped version of the image. With pictures of people, rings and watches appear on the wrong side, as do birthmarks, hair partings, etc. Over the years many magazines and newspapers have received complaints because they have flipped images of recognisable places. This type of inept manipulation of an image is usually pretty obvious. The flipped image of the Houses of Parliament shown in Figure 4.22 for example, clearly has Big Ben on the wrong end of the building. Always check a horizontally flipped image for any telltale signs that it has been altered.

The Flip Canvas Vertical option produces an upside-down version of the image (Figure 4.23), but this is not the same as turning the picture upside-down using 180 degrees of rotation (Figure 4.24). The picture in Figure 4.23 is a "mirror" image of the original, which is demonstrated by the mirrored lettering, whereas the rotated image is not. With this book turned upside-down the nameplate in Figure 4.24 still says "Olympus", but this is clearly not the case with Figure 4.23. Rotation by 180 degrees must therefore be used if you wish to turn an upside-down image the right

Fig.4.23 This image has been flipped vertically

Fig.4.24 Flipping and rotation are not the same

way up. The Flip Canvas Vertical function is mainly used for producing mirrored effects.

Free Transform

So far we have only considered changes applied to the entire image or virtually the entire image, but changes that are only applied to selections are also possible. With an area selected on the image the Edit menu offers a Free Transform option together with various facilities from the Transform submenu (Figure 4.25). The Free Transform option will be considered first, and this can handle most requirements. For the sake of this example it will be assumed that the task is to enlarge the rose near the bottom right-hand corner of Figure 4.26. As the picture stands, interest is divided between the three roses, and there is no main subject. Making one of the roses bigger will effectively bring it forward and make it the dominant element, hopefully giving a stronger composition in the process.

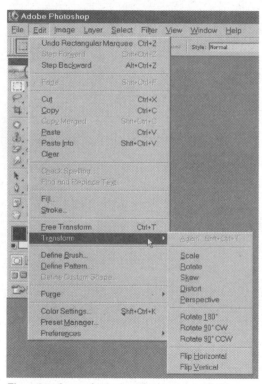

Fig.4.25 A number of options are available from the Transform submenu

The first task is to select the outline of the rose, and was done using the Magic Wand and Marquee tools. Next the Free Transform option is selected from the Edit menu, and the familiar rectangle with eight handles

Fig.4.26 The rose in the bottom-right corner is ready for scaling

Fig.4.27 The rose is larger but the rest of the image is unchanged

Fig.4.28 Here some rotation has been used on the rose

Fig.4.29 Moving the rose to the left has left some blank areas

appears around the selection. It is possible to resize the selection by dragging the handles, and the aspect ratio is not locked. However, it can be locked by holding down the shift key and resizing the selection using one of the four corner handles. Figure 4.27 shows the photograph with the slightly enlarged rose. Bear in mind that Photoshop has to add pixels when a selection is enlarged, but it can not add any detail. Massive amounts of enlargement should not produce outsize pixels, but could still

Fig.4.30 The completed photograph, with the blank areas retouched

produce some rough looking results. Unless the image is a very high resolution type it is best to be conservative when scaling objects up in size.

It is possible to rotate the selection by dragging outside the selection but within the image. Hold down the Shift key to limit rotation to 15 degree increments. Some rotation has been added in Figure 4.28. It is also possible to move the selection by dragging on any part of it. Figure 4.29 shows the enlarged rose moved to the left. This shows the inevitable problem when moving objects or making them smaller. Space vacated by the object is replaced with the white background. This does not matter too much if the white areas can be easily retouched, but in some cases it could be difficult to do so. In this example the blurred background is easily extended to cover the empty white areas, as in the final version of Figure 4.30.

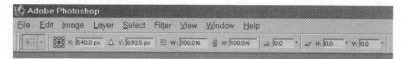

Fig.4.31 The Options bar in the Free Transform mode

With Free Transform selected it is possible to use numeric values to control the size, position and rotation of the selection (Figure 4.31). The image will instantly respond to any changes in these values so that the effect can be seen. The two values on the extreme right enable the selection to be skewed horizontally or vertically. A substantial amount of horizontal skewing has been added to one of the roses in Figure 4.32.

The icon near the left end of the Options bar enables the reference point to be moved from the centre to one of the eight handles. Any rotation for example, will be centred on the reference point. To move the reference point simply left-click on the appropriate handle of the button's icon. In effect, each of the nine handles is a separate and very small button.

Fig.4.32 This distortion was produced using horizontal skewing

*Fig.4.33 The reference point is the the left of the image near the
bottom of the screen*

There is a marker within the selection that shows the reference point,
and it can be freely moved by dragging it to the desired position. Using
this method it is possible to have the reference point anywhere on the
image, or even outside the image, as in Figure 4.33.

Transform submenu

Using the options in the Transform submenu it is possible to rotate, scale,
and skew the selection, in much the same way as when using the Free
Transform method. The main difference is that only one of these can be
applied at a time. If Rotation is selected, a handle appears in each corner
of the selection marquee, but it can not be used to alter the size of the
selection. It can only be rotated or moved by dragging within the selection
box. While restricting the editing to one type at a time is relatively slow,
it has the advantage that it is not possible to accidentally change one
parameter while editing another. Incidentally, there is no Move option in
the Transform submenu, because the selection can still be dragged in
the normal way when using the other options. Note that the Transform

Fig.4.34 Masses amounts of distortion can be produced using skewing

submenu also offers straightforward rotations by 90 and 180 degrees as separate rotation options.

With the Skew option selected it is possible to control the amount of skewing via the Options bar or by dragging the handles. It is possible to produce massive amounts of distortion by dragging the handles, as can be seen from the example of Figure 4.34. Of course, when skewing is applied to items in an image it is usually to make things that are a bit out of shape look somewhat better. The smallest of the three flower heads in the rose photograph has drooped slightly out of shape at the front, and it has been beautified slightly in Figure 4.35 by using some skewing. The background has then been retouched to fill in the areas where areas of white had been left.

The Again option simply repeats the previous transformation. You can make a new selection and then repeat the previous transformation on the new selection. This is useful where several objects require exactly the same processing. It is not usually possible to select all the objects and then apply the transformation en masse. Two or more selections

Fig.4.35 The smallest rose has been beautified using skewing

effectively become one big selection, with a single selection box drawn around them (Figure 4.36). Any processing applied is then referenced to a single point, which might be what is required. In many cases though, processing such as rotation is required around the centre of each selection, and not around a common point. The processing then has to be individually applied to each object. The Again option provides a quick and easy means of applying this type of transformation to a number of objects.

Distort

A Distort option is offered in addition to skewing. The two are similar, but there are no restrictions on the placement of the handles using the Distort function. The Distort option would probably the better one for something like the reshaping of the rose, due to the greater freedom that it provides. Skewing is probably used most where converging verticals are a problem with one object in a scene rather than an entire scene. This can sometimes happen with interior shots, particularly if a wide-angle lens is

Fig.4.36 One transformation box applied to three selections (the roses)

used. As always, it is a matter of using whichever editing technique you find the easiest to use for a given task.

There is a Perspective option in the Transform submenu, and this can also be used to correct perspective problems. In common with the other transformations it can be applied selectively or globally. In Figure 4.37 it has been applied to the entire photograph of Boadicea's statue and Big Ben. Moving the bottom left handle inwards has resulted in the one at the bottom right also moving inwards by the same amount. This obviously makes life much easier if the perspective problem is symmetrical. In Figure 4.38 the Enter key has been operated and the perspective correction has been applied. In this case the original method was probably better since symmetrical correction has not completely "straightened" both sides of the photograph.

The Perspective function is not limited to perspective correction, and it can be used to deliberately exaggerate perspective. This has been done in Figure 4.39 where the statue and tower have effectively been stretched vertically. Slightly more subtly perhaps, in Figure 4.40 the rose in the

Fig.4.37 Applying a change in the perspective

Fig.4.38 The converging verticals have been largely corrected

Fig.4.39 Perspective can be deliberately exaggerated

bottom part of the photograph has been distorted so that it appears to be facing upwards rather more than in the original version. It is well worthwhile experimenting with the various perspective functions, which have a great deal of creative potential in addition to their use for correcting things like converging verticals. Use whichever one you find best for a given situation.

Liquify

The Liquify function is found in the Filter menu in the current version of Photoshop, but it is not exactly a filter. On the other hand, it is not a normal form of transformation function either. A new window appears when this function is selected, and the images can then be smeared to produce all sorts of strange distortions (Figure 4.41). I do not know if this has any serious applications, but it is mainly used in the production of joke images or just for the fun of it.

Fig.4.40 The bottom rose appears to have a greater upward tilt

As one final point on transformations, do not forget that both types of flip transformation are available for selections. Figure 4.42 is the picture with the enlarged rose, but the large rose has been selected again and flipped horizontally. The vacant areas of background that this left have been repaired. The large rose now faces towards the left instead of to

Fig.4.41 The Liquify filter is something less than subtle

the right. This is probably not the type of thing that you will use everyday, but it can sometimes be used to improve composition of a picture. An advantage of selective flipping is that it is less likely to leave telltale signs than flipping the entire image. It is still necessary to take due care to avoid mirrored writing or any other obvious clues that part of the image has been flipped.

Paths

When vector graphics are added to images using the shape tools, pen tool, etc., the lines produced are paths in Photoshop terminology. They are called paths rather than lines because they are not visible on printouts or exported images. Paths can be made visible by adding strokes or fills. Strokes make the paths visible as lines. Fills are used with shapes to make the shape visible, but the paths remain invisible unless stokes are added as well. It is possible to convert paths into selections or vice versa. Turning paths into selections will be considered first.

Fig.4.42 The large rose has been flipped horizontally

This might seem pointless, but bear in mind that the Marquee tools only enable some very basic shapes unless you are prepared to draw freehand with the Lasso tool. Editing selections is difficult due to a lack of any proper editing facilities. It is possible to do some crude editing by adding to or subtracting from selections, but this type of thing is not well suited

Fig.4.43 The heart shape was added using the Custom Shape tool

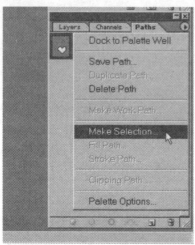

Fig.4.44 The Paths menu

to some applications. There is also a Transform Selection option in the Select menu that enables rotation and scaling to be performed, but this is again not well suited to all applications.

As will be explained later in this chapter, Photoshop can be used in another mode that permits easier editing using the Brush and Eraser tools, and this is worth considering as an alternative to the conversion approach. In general Photoshop offers more than one solution to a problem, and this is certainly the case with masks and selections. This can make the whole subject a bit confusing at first, but it is worthwhile putting some effort into this aspect of the program. All kinds of new possibilities open up once you are proficient at dealing with selections, masks and paths.

Anyway, using the path tools it is possible to produce complex shapes with reasonable ease, and having produced a basic shape it can be edited using relatively sophisticated means. Therefore, with awkward selections it might be easier to draw around the object using the path tools, do any necessary editing, and then convert the path to a selection, rather than using the selection tools. If you require a mask in a fancy shape it is almost certain to be easier to draw it using the path tools and then convert it to a selection.

Path to selection

For this example a heart shape mask will be used on the rose photograph to produce the basis of a Valentine card. Figure 4.43 shows the rose photograph loaded into Photoshop and the heart shape in place on one of the roses. The heart was produced using the Custom Shape tool and one of the built-in shapes, but the conversion process is the same regardless of how the shape is produced. As can be seen from the Layers palette near the bottom right-hand corner of the screen, the new shape has been placed on a new layer.

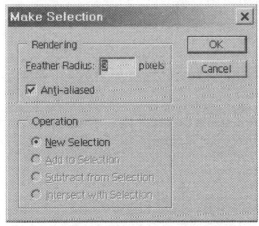

Fig.4.45 The Make Selection dialogue box offers a few settings

The next task is to convert the outline of the shape into a selection. This is done by going to the Paths palette where path for the new shape should be listed. If there is more than one path listed, left-click on the appropriate entry to select it. Next, left-click on the triangle near the top right-hand corner of the Paths palette, which will produce the popup menu of Figure 4.44. Choose the Make Selection

Fig.4.46 The shape and the selection are separate entities

option from this menu. The small dialogue box of Figure 4.45 will then appear, giving the option of altering the Feathering value. It also enables anti-aliasing to be switched on or off. For most purposes the default settings will suffice, but changes can be made where appropriate. Operate the OK button to go ahead and make the selection.

This does not produce much change in the appearance of the image, but the outline should have the familiar flashing pixels of a marquee. The shape and the outline are separate entities, as demonstrated by Figure 4.46 where the shape has been moved slightly, leaving the marquee in place. Having served its purpose the shape is no longer needed and must be deleted. Left-click on the shape using the

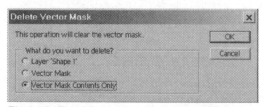

Fig.4.47 The third option is used to delete the shape

Fig.4.48 The area outside the heart shape has been deleted

Path Selection tool and then operate the Delete key. This produces the small dialogue box of Figure 4.47, which provides some control over what is deleted. In this case it is the selection (mask) contents that are not required, so the third option (Vector Mask Contents Only) is selected.

This leaves the mask, but it is on a different layer to the image. This is corrected by

Fig.4.49 Using a higher feathering value (12)

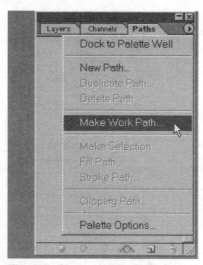

Fig.4.50 Choose Make Work Path

selecting Flatten from the Layer menu, so that the two layers are merged into one. In order to leave the interior of the mask intact and delete everything else it is necessary to use the Inverse option in the Select menu. This results in everything outside the mask rather than everything inside it being selected. Operating the Delete key then leaves the heart shaped crop of the rose (Figure 4.48). It is then a matter of cropping the page down to size and adding the text to complete the home-made card. This type of thing often looks better with a soft focus effect at the edges, which can be achieved using a higher

feathering value when making the selection. Figure 4.49 shows another attempt made using a feathering value of 12, which gives quite a good effect in the original colour version, but probably looks less impressive in greyscale.

Selection to path

A conversion from a selection to a path is useful if you need to draw a complex shape and are fortunate enough to have an image that contains

Fig.4.51 Lower tolerance values give greater accuracy

that shape. Provided the required outline can be produced easily using the Lasso and Magic Wand tools, the conversion method will probably be quicker than drawing it using the path tools. Paths can also be used as a means of saving selections that can be used at some later time, and used as often as necessary.

Note that selections are not saved with images. Fortunately, if you have spent an eternity making an awkward selection and wish to preserve it

Fig.4.52 A tolerance value of 2 has give quite good accuracy

so that you can do some more editing later, the selection can be saved and opened separately. Use the Save Selection option in the Select menu to save it to disc. With the image opened in Photoshop, the selection can be restored using the Load Selection option. The image must be saved in Photoshop's own PSD format for this to work.

In order to convert a selection to a path, first make sure that the Paths palette is visible. Choose the Paths option from the Window menu if this palette is not already on the screen. Select the appropriate path if there is more than one listed. Next, left-click the triangular button near the top right-hand corner of the palette, and then select Make Work Path from the popup menu (Figure 4.50). A small dialogue box like the one in Figure 4.51 will appear. Only one setting is available here, and it is the tolerance value in pixels. This determines how closely the path will follow the selection, with small values giving greater accuracy.

Figure 4.52 shows the result with the default setting of 2, and in most places it has followed the selection very accurately. In a few places the rose petals have been clipped at the edges, and a setting of 1 would

Fig.4.53 A high tolerance value gives smooth but approximate results

probably have been better. The minimum valid value is 0.5 incidentally. Figure 4.53 shows the result with a tolerance value of 10. This gives a very smooth outline that is free from jagged edges, but the path is only an approximation of the original selection. It errs significantly inside and outside the area covered by the rose.

Quick masks

Quick masks are a very useful form of mask that make it easier to "fine tune" a selection. In the normal operating mode it is only possible adjust a selection by adding to it or subtracting from it using the selection tools. This may be sufficient to rapidly tidy up any rough edges or other imperfections, but it is often a cumbersome way of handling things. It would be easier if selections could be enlarged using the Brush tool or reduced using the Eraser tool. This method of adjustment is possible by switching to the Quick Mask mode. There are two buttons in the Toolbox just beneath the Colour buttons, and operating the one on the right places

Fig.4.54 Photoshop in Quick Mask mode with the large rose selected

Photoshop in Quick Mask mode. Operating the button on the left returns Photoshop to the Standard mode.

If there is already a selection, this will be shown normally in Quick Mask mode and the rest of the image will be covered with a 50 percent red tint (Figure 4.54). This will not show up well on all images, and is clearly inappropriate for images or selections that are predominantly red. Double-clicking the Quick Mask button produces the dialogue box of Figure 4.55 where the colour and opacity of the tint can be altered.

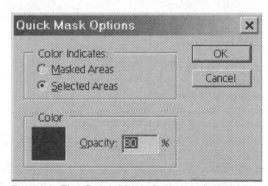

Fig.4.55 The Quick Mask Options window

Fig.4.56 A few imperfections appear with the rose masked

The original red tint did not work well with the rose photograph, and an 80 percent black tint was used for Figure 4.54.

The non-selected area is tinted by default, and this is good at showing up errors where the selection is generally too large. In this example the selection is generally a fraction too small, and having the selection tinted shows the errors more clearly (Figure 4.56). The parts of the rose that have been missed by the selection process stand out well against the dark mask and background, and seem to glow. In this example the original selection was quite accurate, but there are a few small islands and some of the edges have been missed, particularly on the left-hand side.

Use the Brush tool to add to the mask or the Eraser tool to remove parts of it. In Figure 4.57 the Brush tool has been used to remove the more obvious imperfections in the mask. A hole has been added in the mask to show how it can be edited using the Eraser tool. The mask is converted back to a selection when Photoshop is returned to the Standard mode. This is demonstrated by Figure 4.58, where Photoshop has been returned

Fig.4.57 The ouline improved and a hole added to the mask

to Standard mode and the selection has been deleted. In this example there was only one selection, but the system works in exactly the same fashion with multiple selections. If there is no selection when Quick Mask mode is entered, a mask or masks can be "painted" on the screen from scratch. In fact new masks can be produced in this way even if there were selections when Quick Mask mode was entered.

Creating paths

Creating and editing paths using the Pen tool, etc., will probably be reasonably straightforward if you are used to programs such as CorelDraw! and Adobe Illustrator. It will almost certainly seem more than a little strange if you are not familiar with illustration programs. Some of the drawing tools will probably seem as though they produce random lines and squiggles. It can certainly take a while to get used to drawing and editing tools of this type. For initial experiments with the Pen tool it is best to start with a fresh canvas. Select the New option from the file

*Fig.4.58 Back in Standard mode the selected area has been deleted,
showing that the selection was indeed modified*

menu and choose a canvas size that gives plenty of room for
experimentation.

Fig.4.59 A shape produced from five points

Try selecting the
standard Pen tool and
left-clicking at a few
points on the screen.
This produces a
series of straight lines
that go from one click
point to the next, and
from the final point
back to the
beginning. I tried
placing five points on
the canvas and
obtained the result
shown in Figure 4.59.
The outline is

automatically filled with the current foreground colour, but a different colour can be selected by left-clicking the Color button on the Options bar. This produces the Color Picker where the required colour is selected in the usual way. Note that this changes the fill colour but does not change the current foreground colour. The reason that shapes rather than

Fig.4.60 A straight edge can be converted into a curve

lines are produced is that the Pen tool defaults to the Shape Layer mode. The three buttons near the left end of the Options bar offer this and two other modes, and further buttons offer variations on the Pen tool such as shape tools. For the moment, use the Shape Layers mode and the standard Pen tool.

A small cross appears next to the pointer when it is positioned very close to an edge of the shape. This indicates that the straight edge can be dragged into a curve, as in Figure 4.60. There are two new additions here, which are the control point on the path, and a straight line that controls the curve that has been introduced into the path. The angle of the control line sets the angle path at the control point. The length of the line sets the amount of curvature. A long line produces a much more pronounced curve than a short one. In Figure 4.60 the left mouse button has not been released yet, and the original fill appears on the screen. The fill automatically adjusts to the new shape when the mouse button is released.

Direct Selection tool

Initially the control line is centred on the control point, but using the Direct Selection tool it is possible to individually adjust the lengths of the two sections. In Figure 4.61 the lower part of the line has been shortened, and this has reduced the amount of curvature in the part of the path

Fig.4.61 *The lines control the amount of curvature*

controlled by that section of the control line. The line is setting the angle of the path at the control point. One section of the line controls the amount of curvature leading into the control point, and the other section controls the degree of curvature on the other side of the control point.

This type of curve is known as a Bezier curve. A French gentleman of that name, who required a means of drawing complex curves using a computer, invented Bezier curves. He apparently needed them as an aid to designing vehicles for a French manufacturer that produced particularly curvy cars at that time. However, the versatility of Bezier curves is such that they can be used when drawing just about anything. They form the basis of most modern vector graphics programs.

Fig.4.62 *The control points can be moved*

More editing

Using the Direct Selection tool it is possible to control more than the control lines for Bezier curves. In Figure 4.62 for example, the ends of the lines have been dragged to new positions. The control points can also be dragged using the Pen tool while the Control key is

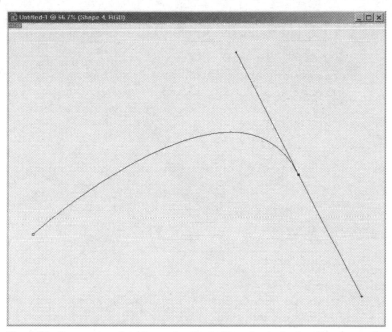

Fig.4.63 Curves can be drawn by dragging when placing the second end of the path

operated. You do not have to draw a series of straight lines and edit them into curves. To draw a curved line, start by left-clicking at the start point, and then drag a line at a different part of the screen. This should produce something like Figure 4.63, and the line dragged onto the screen is the control line for the second end of the path. I have set the fill colour to match the background so that the lines can be seen clearly with no fill to confuse matters.

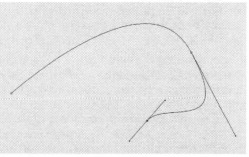

Fig.4.64 Another section has been added

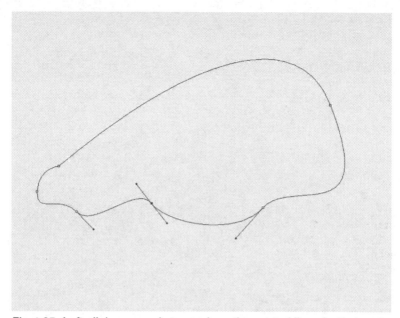

Fig.4.65 Left-click on a node to produce the control lines for that part of the curve

Once on the screen the curve can be edited using the Direct Selection tool, or another section can be added using the Pen tool (Figure 4.64). Of course, straight sections and curves can be freely mixed. Left-click to add a straight segment or drag a control line to produce a new curved section. In order to edit curves using the Direct Selection tool it is first necessary to left-click near one of the nodes. This produces the control line for that node, plus the one on each side of it (Figure 4.65), and gives full control over the curve on either side of the node.

In addition to moving the control points and directly adjusting the control lines, the entire shape can be moved using the Path Selection tool. Simply drag the shape to the new position, making sure that you starting dragging from within the shape. Using the Direct Selection tool it is possible to drag a straight section of the outline to a new position. Start the dragging operation at any point on the straight line that you wish to move. This does not operate in the same way with curved sections, where it has the effect of increasing or decreasing the amount of curvature. The ends of the lines do not move.

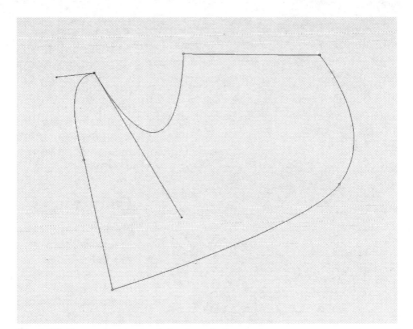

Fig.4.66 An angle can be introduced at a node

Operating the Shift key restricts the movement of control points and lines to 45 degree increments. Holding down the Control key while dragging on a shape or path produces a copy that can be dragged away from the original to a new position. Operating the Alt key while adjusting a control line enables the two sections of the line to be set at different

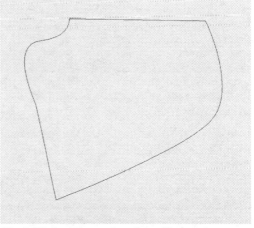

Fig.4.67 A path can be closed to produce a shape

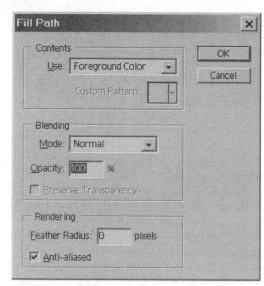

Fig.4.68 A number of options are available when adding a fill to a path

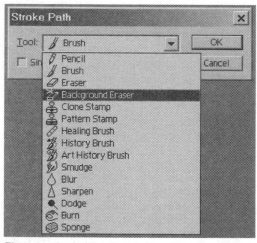

Fig.4.69 Any of the brush based tools can be used when adding strokes

angles, as in Figure 4.66. The angle of the path is normally the same on both sides of a control point, but using this method it is possible to have different angles and introduce an abrupt change of angle into a curve.

Paths mode

The Pen tool operates in a similar fashion in the Paths mode, but no fill is applied. A shape can be produced by finishing the final section on the start point, as in Figure 4.67. The lines are edited in the same way as the outlines of shapes in the Shape Layers mode. Closed shapes can be filled by selecting the path and then activating the popup menu of the Paths palette. Selecting Fill Path produces the dialogue box of Figure 4.68 which gives a range of options. By default the shape is filled with the current foreground colour, but there are other

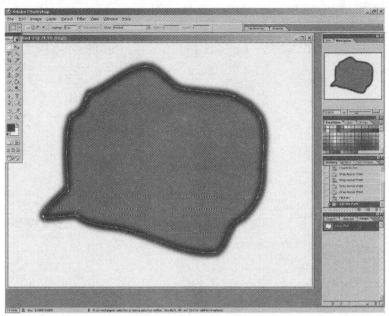

Fig.4.70 *A stroke and a fill have been added to this closed path*

options such as the background colour or a pattern. Where necessary, the opacity and feathering values can be adjusted.

Paths can be turned into lines in a similar fashion. Select the appropriate path and then activate the popup menu of the Paths palette, where the Stroke Path option is chosen. This produces the dialogue box of

Fig.4.71 *This path was produced using the Freeform Pen tool*

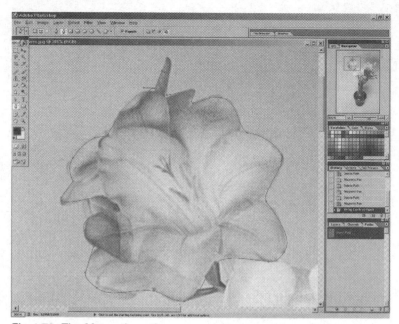

Fig.4.72 The Magnetic option was used to trace this outline

Figure 4.69 where any of the brush type tools can be selected. For most purposes the standard Brush tool will suffice. Note that the brush used to paint over the path will be whichever one is currently selected for the brush tool that you select. Remember to select the correct brush before using the Stroke Path facility. Figure 4.70 shows a path that has been filled and has also had a stroke added.

Freeform Pen

The Freeform Pen tool is a useful alternative to the standard version. Using this tool it is possible to draw freehand onto the canvas, but the path that is drawn is a series of Bezier curves and not a line of pixels. This point is demonstrated by Figure 4.71 where a shape has been drawn onto the screen and the path has then been selected. The control points and some of the control lines can be seen in Figure 4.71. The path is easily edited if it is not exactly as required. The control points and lines can be manipulated in the normal fashion. In general, it is easier to

Fig.4.73 A few seconds of editing was sufficient to give much more accurate results

produce a shape using the Freeform Pen tool than it is using the standard Pen tool, particularly if you are new to Bezier curves.

The Freeform Pen tool can be used to trace over shapes in an image, but this is often easier if the Magnetic checkbox on the Options bar is ticked. The Freeform Pen tool then operates in a manner that is similar to the Magnetic Lasso tool, with the path following contrasts in the image. The triangular button just to the left of the checkbox activates a pop-down menu that gives essentially the same options that are available when using the Magnetic Lasso tool. Figure 4.72 shows a photograph of a flower where the magnetic option has been used to trace around the outline. As normal with this type of thing, the path has deviated from the outline in a few places, but this is easily corrected via the control points and lines. A few seconds of editing produced the more accurate version of Figure 4.73.

Overlapping

When using the Pen tools there are four buttons on the Options bar that determine how overlapping shapes and paths interact. These operate in the same fashion as their equivalents for selections. Note that shapes produced using the shape tools have outlines that are comprised of Bezier curves, and that they can be edited in the normal ways using the Direct Selection and Path Selection tools. Try drawing an ellipse using the Ellipse tool and then select it using the Direct Path tool. You will find that it consists of four Bezier curves that can be edited in the normal way.

You may wish to add some shapes to the menu of custom shapes, and this is easily done. Select the shape using the Path tool and the select the Define Custom Shape option from the Edit menu. Add a suitable name for the shape in the textbox of the window that pops-up (Figure 4.74), and then operate the OK button

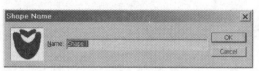

Fig.4.74 Add a suitable name in the textbox

to add the shape to the menu. Select the Custom Shape tool and check that the shape has been added at the bottom of the current shape menu.

Selections, paths, and masks are a bit bewildering due to the enormous range of tools and functions associated with them. It is well worthwhile spending some time learning at least a few of the basics though. Photoshop's capabilities are greatly enhanced even if you only understand the selection tools and the Quick Mask mode. If you can become fluent using paths as well, then so much the better.

Points to remember

If there is a selection or several selections on the image, processing such as changes in contrast and brightness will only be applied to the selected areas. With nothing selected, changes to things like colour balance and brightness are applied to the whole image. Some processing, such as transformations, can only be applied to selections.

Selections can be moved to another part of the image, but a "hole" will be left in the area that the material used to occupy. This can usually be healed using the Clone tools and normal retouching techniques.

Unwanted material near the edges of an image can be removed using the Crop tool. The Crop tool can also be used to level sloping horizons, correct converging verticals, and deliberately introduce distortions.

Flipping the whole image or a selection can improve the composition of a picture or make it fit into a page layout in a more satisfactory fashion. However, unless due care is taken it is often obvious that an image has been flipped. Flipping does not work with any images that contain text, famous places, and even pictures of people can give problems.

The Quick Mask mode effectively enables selections to be "painted" onto the screen and trimmed back using the Eraser tool. Existing selections can be edited using the Brush and Eraser tools. This is often the quickest means of "fine tuning" a selection that has gone slightly awry.

Shapes and paths consist of straight lines and Bezier curves that are easily edited. Paths can be converted into selections and selections can be converted into paths. Paths do not have a fill or even produce lines on an image unless the Fill Path and (or) Stroke Path facilities are used.

Bezier curves are controlled by two lines, one at each end. The angles of the lines set the start and finish angles of the curves. The lengths of the lines set the degree of curvature in their respective sections of the curve. Virtually any shape can be produced using Bezier curves and straight lines.

Especially for inexperienced users, the Freeform Pen tool represents an easy way of getting basic shapes into Photoshop. The shapes are comprised of Bezier curves that can be edited in the normal way. Using the magnetic option enables shapes in an image to be traced very easily, and any imperfections are easily corrected.

Colour mixing

Mixing it

With a program like Photoshop there are two main aspects to colour, which are mixing a colour to use when drawing or painting on the screen, and adjusting the colour balance of the image. Corrections to the colour balance are often applied to the entire picture, but if necessary they can be applied to selections. Adjusting the colour balance is much easier if you already understand colour mixing, so we will start with the mixing process.

There is an obvious problem when discussing colour in a book that is printed in black and white. There is no way of showing colours or changes in colour. Even if this book was printed in colour, there is no guarantee that the colour reproduction would be accurate enough to illustrate the points properly. In order to follow the material in this chapter you really need to have Photoshop up and running on your PC so that you can try things for yourself and see the results of adjusting the colour controls. It is a good idea to do things this way with all the subjects covered in this book, but it is especially important when dealing with colour. Remember that the free demonstration version has a full range of features, and is all you need in order to try any aspect of Photoshop yourself.

Colour models

Photoshop handles colour via four colour models, which are ways of producing the wide range of colours used in images. These are the four colour models:

RGB (red, green, blue)

CMYK (cyan, magenta, yellow, black)

HSB (hue, saturation, brightness)

CIE Lab

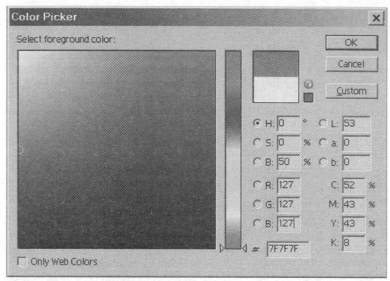

Fig.5.1 *The Color Picker provides the main means of selecting colours*

There are various modes for handling colour, but you need to gain a basic understanding of the models before going on to these. One way of mixing or picking colours with Photoshop is to use the Color Picker (Figure 5.1). The Color Picker can be launched by left-clicking on the foreground or background squares near the bottom of the Toolbox. It is then used to choose a new foreground or background colour, depending on which button was operated. The Color Picker can be launched from certain other sources, such as from the Options bar when using the Pen tool to produce shapes. The function of the colour selected by the Color Picker depends on the context in which it is used, and in this example it is used to choose the fill colour for the shapes being produced.

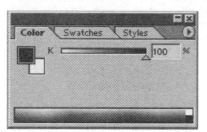

Fig.5.2 *The Color palette is simpler than the Color Picker*

There is also a Color palette (Figure 5.2), which may already be present on the screen. If not, it can be displayed by selecting Color from the Window menu. The bar along the bottom of the Color palette is essentially the same as the one down the middle of the Color Picker. Placing the pointer over the bar in the Color palette results in the pointer automatically changing into the eyedropper tool. Left-clicking on a colour in the bar results in that colour being used in the Color Picker. The same method can be used with the bar in the Color Picker, but the pointer does not change to the eyedropper icon. The colour can also be changed by dragging the pointers on opposite sides of the bar in the Color Picker.

RGB

RGB is the system used to produce the colours on televisions and computer monitors. In theory at any rate, a full range of colours can be produced by mixing these three primary colours at the right intensities. Photoshop uses 24-bit RGB colour, with eight bits being used for each primary colour. For each primary colour this gives 256 different intensities from 0 (off) to 255 (maximum). The total number of colours available is 256 x 256 x 256, which works out nearly 16.8 million different colours. Estimates of the number of colours that can be perceived by average human vision vary somewhat. Most seem to put the figure at considerably less than 16.8 million.

Using the same intensity for each colour provides a greyscale that has 254 shades of grey plus black and white. This is more than adequate to produce good black and white images, or greyscale Images as they are more accurately called. You can demonstrate that identical values produce greys by typing the same value for R, G, and B into the appropriate textboxes of the Color Picker. The circle in the large panel in the left-hand section of the Color Picker shows the currently selected colour, and will instantly respond to changes in these values.

The two rectangles near the top of the colour bar show the newly selected colour (top) and the colour that was already in use (bottom). The upper rectangle there responds to changes in the colour values so that you can clearly see newly selected colours. Left-click the lower rectangle if you change your mind and wish to return to the original colour selection.

By using different intensities for the primary colours it is possible to produce a wide range of colours. In theory a full range of colours can be produced, but it pays to bear in mind that real-world monitors and printing systems have some limitations. A huge range of colours can still be produced though, giving convincing results with practically any image. In general with the RGB system, the higher the values used, the lighter the colour that is produced.

CMYK

If you learned to mix colours in art classes at school, you are probably puzzled by the primary colours being red, green, and blue. When mixing paints the primary colours are red, blue and yellow, except red and blue are not really true primary colours. In order to get accurate colours it is necessary to respectively use cyan and magenta instead of blue and red. The primary colours for projected light (as in a monitor) and reflected light (as in painting and colour printers) are different. If you did physics at school, you no doubt did projected light experiments where the primary colours suddenly (and confusingly) became different to the ones used in the art classes.

This is because projected light is additive, and mixing the primary colours therefore produces white, as in the well known physics experiment. Reflected light is subtractive, and mixing the primary colours produces a dark grey colour. Knowing this does not really make matters much less confusing, but as explained shortly, it is possible to select colours in Photoshop without resorting to either method.

By mixing cyan, magenta, and yellow inks or paints it is possible to produce a wide range of colours, but only in middle tones. Some artists obtain lighter tones by mixing white with the basic colour. Watercolorists mostly rely on using white paper and using the paint thinly so that the paper shows through. Colour printers such as inkjet units use the watercolorist method of producing pale colours and, of course, white. Thus, using coloured paper in an inkjet printer produces some odd results.

Dark colours are produced by mixing black with the three primary colours. Four inks (cyan, magenta, yellow, and black) are therefore used in inkjet printers. I assume that K rather than B is used for black in CMYK because B is already used for blue in RGB. Note that some inkjet printers use more than four inks in an attempt to obtain better colour accuracy, but they still use what is essentially the CMYK system. The additional inks are usually lighter versions of cyan and magenta.

HSB

HSB is similar to the CMYK method, but it uses a range of preset colours, or hues. The Photoshop Color Picker seems to be primarily aimed at this method of colour selection. These hues are the colours in the colour bar, and the full rainbow spectrum of colours is included here. The colour value runs from 0 to 359 degrees, and it is based on the positions of colours on a conventional colour wheel. One of the basic colours can be modified by changing its saturation and brightness. Saturation is the purity of the colour, and it is a pure red, blue, or whatever with 100 percent saturation. Lower saturations are produced by mixing neutral grey with the selected colour. This gives a less strong colour, with neutral grey being produced at zero percent saturation.

Note that mixing grey into a colour reduces the strength of the colour, but not its brightness. The latter is controlled via the third setting, and this runs from zero with no brightness (black) to 100 at maximum brightness. Although zero brightness always produces black, maximum brightness does not necessarily produce pure white. If the saturation value is more than 0, some colour will be added to the white. The left-hand panel of the Color Picker shows all the variations for a given hue value.

Colours higher up the panel have greater brightness than those further down. The further to the right, the stronger the colour saturation. This gives black along the bottom of the panel and a greyscale up the left-hand side. Anywhere else there is a true variation on the selected hue. Bright colours with strong saturation are found towards the top right-hand corner, and dark colours with strong saturation are available in the bottom right-hand corner. Colours in the top left-hand corner have weak colour but high brightness, while those in the bottom left-hand corner have low brightness and weak colour content.

This system can be a bit confusing at first, but it is actually very easy to use. Suppose you require a dark but strong blue colour. The saturation must be high to give the strong colour but the brightness must be fairly low in order to produce a suitably dark shade of blue. The likely location of the required colour is therefore about half way up the main panel (about half brightness) and well over to the right (strong colour saturation).

To find the required colour it is a matter of setting the pointers on the colour bar to the middle of the range of blue colours, and then looking at the appropriate area of the main panel. If a suitable colour can not be seen, moving the pointers up and down slightly should produce

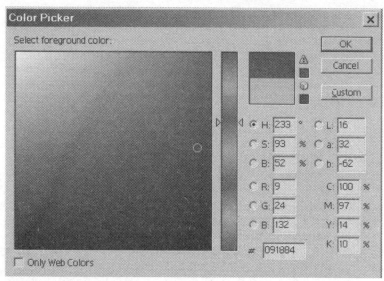

Fig.5.3 The correct blue was produced using more or less the expected settings

something suitable. When a suitable colour is found, left-click on it and look at the appropriate rectangle to the right of the panel, where the selected colour will be displayed. Remember that the upper rectangle shows the currently selected colour, and the lower rectangle shows the colour that was in use previously. Try left-clicking around the initial point to see if a better result can be obtained.

If you find a colour that is close to the one you require, but you would like to experiment further, make a note of the RGB values. You can then go back to that colour at a later time, should you wish to do so. An alternative ploy is to select it by operating the OK button and then go back into the Color Picker. The colour selected previously will then be shown in the lower rectangle to the right of the main colour panel, which is handy for comparison purposes. In order to revert to the previous colour selection, either left-click on the lower rectangle and operate the OK button, or just operate the Cancel button.

As a simple example of colour selection I tried to match the deep blue colour of a pen that happened to be on my computer desk, and Figure 5.3 shows the result. As expected, the required colour was about half way up the main panel and well over to the right. Even if the correct colour was somewhere else on the panel, it would soon be spotted. Once you have a basic understanding of the Color Picker it can be used to quickly produce any required colour.

CIE Lab

The CIE Lab colour model has three parameters, which are the luminance (l) and two colour components (a and b). Colour components a and b respectively cover from red to green and from blue to yellow. It is apparently more wide ranging than the other colour models, but for most users it is definitely not the most convenient to work with. The CIE Lab model will not be considered further here.

Which model?

By default Photoshop uses the RGB colour model, but the others are available from the Mode submenu of the Image menu (Figure 5.4). Unless there is a good reason to do otherwise, it is advisable to settle for the default mode, which is the one used by your monitor. Note that it is not necessary to use (say) CMYK because the final output will be printed via an inkjet printer. Photoshop and the printer's driver software will make the conversion from RGB to CMYK, and within the limitations of the printer the correct colours should be obtained.

There is a Grayscale option available from the Mode submenu, and this can be useful where the final output will be in black and

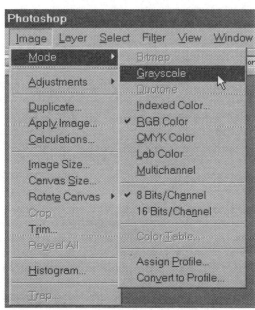

Fig.5.4 The options in the Mode submenu

white even though the original images are colour pictures. The photographs and screen dumps in this book, for example, start out in full glorious colour, but have to be converted to greyscale images. Without this conversion, which is done using the Grayscale option of the Mode submenu, there could be serious problems for the book's printers.

It is not absolutely necessary to use this option where colour images are printed from Photoshop using a monochrome printer such as a laser type. Photoshop and the printer's driver software should make a good job of converting the colour images into good greyscale printouts. The Grayscale mode might still be useful though, since it enables colour images to be previewed in monochrome before printing them out. This gives you a chance to check that the brightness and contrast are satisfactory after the conversion to a greyscale image.

Note that it is not possible to convert a greyscale image back to a colour type. It is possible to revert to the colour image if it is available from the History palette, but it is otherwise lost once the conversion to monochrome has been made. It is advisable to save the image prior to conversion, and then save it again under a different name once it has been converted to a greyscale type. You then have copies of the colour and monochrome versions.

Modes

We have already encountered the Modes menu and one of the modes (Grayscale). There are also RGB, CMYK, and CIE Lab (Lab Color) modes, but no HSB mode. As pointed out previously, modes and colour models are not the same. The modes provide methods for working with the various colour models. When you work with the Grayscale mode the monitor is still operating as a RGB colour monitor and the video card is still operating as a colour type. This is demonstrated by the fact that the title bar at the top of the Photoshop window is still displayed in shades of blue.

It is possible to work with greyscale images in colour mode, but it would be necessary to take great care not to use anything other than neutral grey colours. Image files would be unnecessarily large because (typically) three bytes per pixel would be used, whereas only one is needed for greyscale images. Having Photoshop operate in the Grayscale mode makes life easier for the user. Using the Grayscale mode makes it impossible to use anything other than shades of neutral grey. It also keeps file sizes smaller.

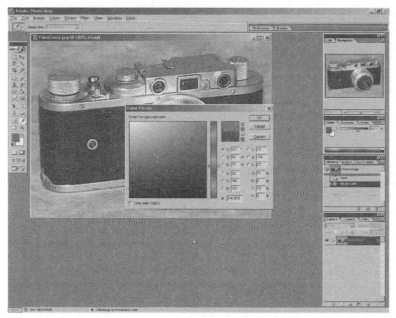

Fig.5.5 The standard Color Picker has appeared in Grayscale mode

Selecting the Color Picker in the greyscale mode does actually produce the standard version of the Color Picker (Figure 5.5), and the colour bar is present in the Color palette. However, using either to select a colour actually results in what Photoshop deems to be an equivalent shade of grey being selected.

When using the Color Picker in the Grayscale mode it is only the shades of grey down the right-hand side of the main colour panel that are of interest.

The situation is similar with the Color palette (Figure 5.6). The usual colour bar is shown at the bottom

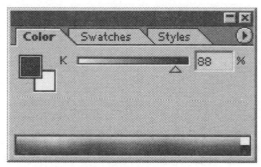

Fig.5.6 The Color palette offers about 100 shades of grey

*Fig.5.7 Converting this image to a bitmap has produced a very coarse
image that lacks detail*

of the palette, but left-clicking on it selects what Photoshop deems to be
the equivalent shade of grey for the chosen colour. The slider control
above the colour bar enables shades of grey from zero percent (white)
to 100 percent (black) to be selected. While this is less than the full 256
shades of grey, 100 shades should suffice for most purposes. The
appropriate colour button in the Toolbox responds to changes in the
setting of the slider control, so you can see clearly the shade that has
been selected. You can switch between foreground and background
control using the two buttons to the left of the slider.

Fig.5.8 This bitmap gives slightly more convincing results

Bitmap

The term bitmap tends to be used for any image that is made up of pixels. In the early days of computing, bitmap images were true bitmaps that used one bit per pixel. The problem in using just one bit of information for each pixel is that it limits each pixel to two states. In other words, each pixel is either black or white, with no shades of grey available. Bitmap images do not necessarily appear to be strictly black and white though.

It is possible to produce a pseudo greyscale from black and white dots using a process known as dithering, but this only works if the dots are small enough to "fool" the eye. The basic technique is to use several dots per pixel. By using a lot of black dots per pixel, what appears to be a dark pixel is produced. Using a few dots per pixel gives what appears to be a light pixel. Dithering works well with something like a monochrome laser printer where the individual dots are so small that they can not be seen by the human eye.

In the Bitmap mode Photoshop can use a form of dithering to produce a pseudo greyscale, but with one dot per pixel it is inevitable that images become greatly simplified when converted to this mode. Figure 5.7 shows the improved version of the photograph with the artist painting a seascape, but it has been converted to a greyscale image and then to a bitmap. Note that it is not possible to convert direct from a colour image to a bitmap type. Clearly a great deal of information has been lost in the conversion, and the converted image is barely recognisable. Simple bitmaps work better with some pictures than with others, and it is rather more convincing when applied to the photograph of the fake Leica camera (Figure 5.8).

Increased pixels

Better results can be obtained by boosting the number of pixels during the conversion. The small dialogue box of Figure 5.9 appears when the Bitmap option is selected. Various types of dithering are available from the Method menu near the bottom of the window. The upper section shows the input and output resolution of the image. The input resolution is the resolution used in the non-converted image, and by default the output figure is exactly the same.

For this example the output resolution was increased from about 245 dots per inch to 1000 dots per inch. The converted image therefore has about 16 dots for each pixel in the original image, giving much more scope for producing a pseudo greyscale using dithering. Figure 5.10 shows the converted image, which clearly has much more detail than the original version of Figure 5.7.

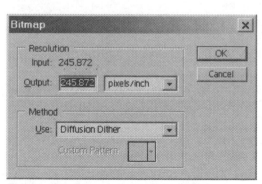

Fig.5.9 The Bitmap dialogue box offers various dithering methods

It is not essential to use any form of dithering in the bitmap mode. Figure 5.11 shows the photograph of Boadicea statue converted to Bitmap mode, but using the 50% Threshold option of the Model menu. This model operates on the simple system of setting a pixel to black or white depending on whether its brightness is above or below 50 percent brightness. The result can be quite dramatic, as in this

Fig.5.10 Boosting the number of pixels has produced better results

case, but it can go seriously wrong. There can be large areas of black and white and the picture might look like nothing much at all. It works best with simple compositions that have good contrast.

When saving a bitmap image you might find that it can not be saved using the original file format. This is simply because some formats do not support something as basic as a true black and white bitmap. One solution is to save the image in a format that does support this type of image, such as TIFF or Photoshop's own PSD format. If you need the image in a format that does not support basic bitmaps, such as Jpeg, the image can be converted back to a greyscale type again. Only two grey levels (black and white) will be used in the converted image though,

Fig.5.11 This image is strictly black and white, with no dithering used

so it will still look the same as the true bitmap. This is demonstrated by Figure 5.12, which is the Jpeg version of the PSD image shown in Figure 5.11.

In order to convert from one mode to another it is merely necessary to select the appropriate mode from the Mode submenu. A tick in this submenu indicates the mode currently in use. If a mode is greyed out it is not possible to convert the image to that mode. Remember that a colour image can be converted to a bitmap type by converting it to a greyscale image first. A warning message will appear if information will be lost by the conversion, such as when turning a colour image into a greyscale type.

Once an image has been saved and then opened again, a conversion can not be reversed if it resulted in information being lost. The situation is different if the image has not been saved and closed. You can go back to the stage prior to conversion if it is still present on the History palette. All is not lost if it has scrolled off the top of the list. Selecting Revert from the File menu will still take the image back to its state immediately prior to conversion. Left-clicking the default snapshot at the top of the History palette will take the image right back to its original state.

Fig.5.12 The Jpeg version of Fig.5.11 looks the same

RGB and CMYK

As already pointed out, RGB is the system used by colour monitors. It is therefore the obvious choice if the final output will be on a computer monitor, such as when producing images for use on the Internet. CMYK is the system used when printing colour images, whether from your own inkjet printer or commercially via expensive professional equipment. Even when producing images that will be printed, many still prefer to work in the RGB mode. The images are then converted to CMYK before they are sent to the printers. There is probably no point in converting images that will be printed from your own inkjet printer. Just use the RGB mode throughout.

When using the CMYK mode you may notice a little warning symbol appear near the left edge of the Color palette when certain colours are selected (Figure 5.13). This is to alert you to the fact that selected colour can not be produced with a high degree of accuracy using the CMYK system. Try selecting New from the file menu to produce a blank canvas, and then use the Brush tool to fill some areas of the canvas with colours that produce the warning symbol. Then select the CMYK mode from the Mode menu and look at the image as the conversion occurs.

Photoshop automatically brings out-of-gamut colours into gamut when converting images to CMYK mode. Incidentally, gamut is simply the range of colours that a system can accommodate. The shift in some colours will probably be quite small, but it will be quite noticeable with others. Try selecting an out-of-gamut colour using the Color palette, and then left-click on the warning symbol or the coloured square just to its right. The warning symbol and square of colour disappear, and the selected colour changes to its equivalent CMYK colour. Incidentally, the same warning symbol appears when the Color Picker is used to produce an out-of-gamut colour.

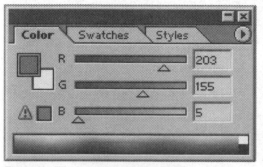

Fig.5.13 The warning symbol is above the left end of the colour bar

It is possible to have the out-of-gamut colours in a RGB image highlighted so that you can see how much of the image will be affected by a conversion to CMYK. Simply select Gamut Warning from the View menu. Figure 5.14 shows one of the rose photographs with this option selected. The out-of-gamut colours are highlighted in white, and many of the stronger pink and orange colours in the flower heads have been highlighted. Select Gamut Warning from the View menu again to switch of the highlighting.

Indexed Color

This mode is used when the final output will be to a device that supports a relatively limited range of colours. These days most monitors and printers support a huge colour range, making the Indexed Color mode of relatively little use. Its main application is probably in the production of images for web pages. The problem in mixing web colours on one computer is that they may be somewhat different when displayed on another computer. One reason for this is simply that different monitors produce different colours from the same colour values. In actual fact, the same monitor will produce different colours depending on how it is set up.

Fig.5.14 The highlighting is most obvious on the smallest rose

A second problem is that not all computers have the same colour capabilities. The main problem here is differences between Macintosh computers and PCs. There can be differences between computers of the same general type, and some PCs have simple graphics cards offering relatively few colours, while others have graphics systems that can handle millions of different colours. However, this is not a major problem these days as even budget PCs and most laptops tend to have good graphics capabilities.

Web safe

It is the Macintosh and PC differences that are of prime concern to most web designers. There is no point in them worrying about poorly adjusted monitors, since there is nothing web designers can do about it. The Macintosh/PC problem is different. There is a set of so-called "browser safe" or "web safe" colours that can be reproduced by the popular Microsoft and Netscape browsers in both their Windows and Macintosh versions. Using these 200 or so colours does not guarantee that precisely

5 Colour mixing

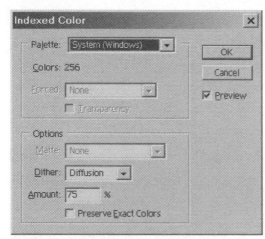

Fig.5.15 The Indexed Color dialogue box

the specified colour will be produced on every computer, but it does at least keep the inevitable divergences to a minimum.

A small dialogue box like the one in Figure 5.15 appears when the Indexed Color mode is selected. In this example Photoshop is running on a PC, so it is the Windows system colours that are offered by default.

Various options are available from the Palette menu though (Figure 5.16), and it is the Web option that provides the web safe colours. If you try converting a colour photograph to this mode it will probably not look much different after the conversion. This is perhaps a little surprising when one considers that the maximum number of colours on the screen

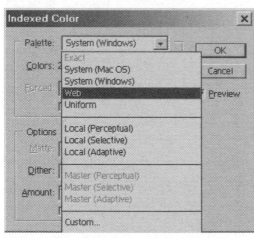

Fig.5.16 The options in the Palette menu

has been probably been reduced from millions to just 216.

The reason for the lack of change is that Photoshop uses dithering in an attempt minimise any change in appearance. Zooming in will often reveal the dithering, with the smooth changes in colour being replaced by a noticeable pattern. Figures 5.17 and 5.18 respectively show

Fig.5.17 The original version of the photograph

Fig.5.18 Results are coarser and grainier in the web safe version

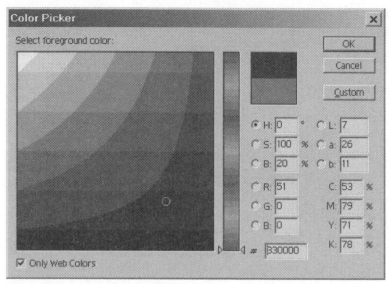

Fig.5.19 The Color Picker with its more restricted colour range

close-up "before" and "after" views of the rose photograph. Although the dithering is obvious on close inspection, it is usually something less than obvious with the image viewed at normal size, which is really all you need to be concerned about with web images.

When using the Indexed Color mode with web safe colours, the Color Picker will not automatically limit the selection to web safe colours. However, it will do so if the Only Web Colors checkbox near the bottom left-hand corner of the window is ticked. Figure 5.19 shows the Color Picker with this option enabled.

Whether it is worth bothering with web safe colours when producing photographic images is debatable. Slightly improved colour accuracy may well be obtained, but only at the expense of somewhat grainier images. This is a subjective matter that you have to judge for yourself. I prefer not to bother with web safe colours for images that will be used on the Internet.

Greyscale to colour

It is worth noting that it is possible to convert a greyscale image to a colour type such as RGB. This might seem pointless, since the converted

image will still be a
black and white type,
and colours will not
miraculously appear
after the conversion.
However, once the
image is a colour type
it is possible to add
coloured text, adjust
the colour balance to
produce a sepia effect
like the one used for
old photographic
prints, add colour to
parts of the image to

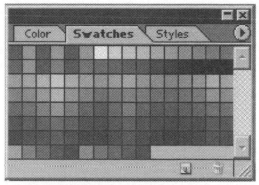

Fig.5.20 The Swatches palette

make them stand out, and so on. You can even try colouring the image
to make it look like a genuine colour image.

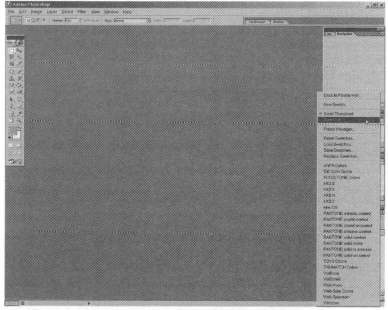

Fig.5.21 The Swatches palette has a large popup menu

Swatches palette

The Swatches palette (Figure 5.20) is normally grouped with the Color palette, and it can be activated by operating the appropriate tab in this group. Alternatively, it can be launched by selecting Swatches from the

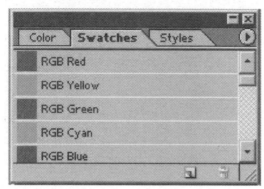

Fig.5.22 The Small List version of the palette

Window menu. It provides quick access to a range of preset colours and a basic greyscale. You can add and delete colours, or even produce your own swatches. If you use certain colours frequently it makes sense to add them to the Swatches palette so that they are almost instantly available.

By default the colours are shown in small thumbnail form. In other words, there is just a small square for each of the colours. Left-clicking on the triangle near the top right-hand corner of the palette produces a large

Fig.5.23 Enter a name for the colour

popup menu (Figure 5.21). Selecting the Small List option changes the Swatches palette to look like Figure 5.22. As before, there is a square that shows the

relevant colour, but there is also a name or short description beside each colour. This is useful where it is necessary to have a range of similar colours. Having a name for each colour should help to avoid confusion.

Adding a colour to the standard swatch is very easy. First select the required colour using the Color Picker or copy it from an image using the Eyedropper tool. With the required colour set as the current foreground colour, place the pointer over an unused square in the Swatches palette. The pointer is the eyedropper icon when it is over one of the occupied squares, but it should switch over to the paint bucket icon when it is over an unused square. Left-click the mouse once the pointer is in position, and a small window like the one of Figure 5.23 will then appear. There will be a default name in the textbox, but this can be edited to something more meaningful.

Operate the OK button when the name has been changed, and a square for the new colour will be added to the Swatches palette. Figure 5.24 shows the Swatches

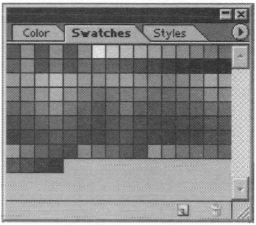

Fig.5.24 10 new colours have been added to the Swatches palette

palette with a range of turquoise blues added. Removing a swatch is very easy, and it is just a matter of dragging it to the Trashcan icon in the bottom right-hand corner of the Swatches palette. Alternatively, right-click on the swatch you wish to remove and then select Delete Swatch from the popup menu that appears.

Channels

Models and modes were covered earlier in this chapter, and it is perhaps worth mentioning a related term you will encounter with Photoshop. Channels are individual elements in a colour mode. For example, the channels when using the RGB mode are red, green, and blue. Photoshop often permits individual control of each channel in addition to overall control.

Wrong colour

Sometimes when using the Eyedropper tool to pick a colour from an image the colour obtained does looks very different to the area of colour that you selected. Making several attempts to select the colour can produce a series of totally different results! The reason for these discrepancies is that an area that appears to be filled with more of less the same colour actually contains a complex pattern of colours. In some cases the pattern of colours is real, but you do not normally look close enough to notice it. Often the problem is caused by an image that has been scanned from a newspaper or magazine, and the multi-coloured dots are simply part of the printing process. Many colour printing processes use dithering plus a few colours to give the illusion of a full colour range.

With the default setting the Eyedropper tool samples a single pixel at the point on the screen that was left-clicked. Results are often better if it is set to sample either a 3 by 3 or 5 by 5 block of pixels. When sampling a block of pixels the colour produced is the average of all the pixels sampled. The sample setting can be altered by right-clicking somewhere on the image with the Eyedropper tool selected. Then select the required option from the popup menu. Rather than repeatedly left-clicking when searching for the right colour, try dragging the Eyedropper tool while looking at the foreground colour in the Toolbox. The colour of this rectangle will change as the Eyedropper tool is dragged around the image, making it easier to find the required colour.

Points to remember

Colour modes and colour models are not quite the same thing. Colour models are the systems used to define colours, such as RGB and CMYK. Colour modes are the means by which Photoshop handles colours, but they are based on the models.

The primary colours are different for the RGB and CMYK systems. CMYK uses the same primary colours that artists use when mixing paint. These are cyan, magenta and yellow, which are more accurate primary colours than the blue, red, and yellow we all used at school. Red, green, and blue are the primary colours for projected light, which is additive rather than subtractive.

The Color Picker is the main tool for selecting colours in Photoshop. Regardless of the mode in use, it uses what is essentially the HSB (hue, saturation, and brightness) approach to colour mixing. You choose a basic colour (hue) and then select a version of it that has the required strength (saturation) and brightness.

The Color palette is a simplified version of the Color Picker, and it is a quick alternative that is adequate for many purposes. There is also a Swatch palette that has a range of preset colours. Any colours that you use frequently can be added to the Swatch palette.

It is possible to work in a colour mode when dealing with greyscale images, but it is best to use the Grayscale mode unless there is a good reason to do otherwise. Working in the Grayscale mode helps to keep file sizes small and ensures that colour can not be accidentally introduced into the image. Of course, a colour mode must be used if you intend to add colour to a greyscale image.

Bitmaps are strictly black and white with no shades in-between. However, a pseudo greyscale can be produced using dithering. This effectively reduces the resolution of the image though.

A range of so-called "web safe" or "browser safe" colours are available, and these ensure reasonable colour accuracy in web applications. Although these provide just over 200 colours, a greater range can effectively be produced using dithering. This can produce slightly grainy looking results.

Colour images can be converted to the greyscale variety. It is not essential to do this before printing a colour image on a black and white printer. However, it is a good idea to do so, as it is then possible to make final adjustments to the brightness and contrast so that the printed image is exactly as required. Remember to keep a colour copy of the image file.

The Eyedropper tool can be used to select any colour in an image. With some images the Eyedropper tool provides better results using an averaging mode, where a block of nine or 25 pixels are sampled. By default it samples a single pixel.

Colour balance

Digital advantages

Some of the advantages of digital imaging have already been covered, such as the ease with which converging verticals and sloping horizons can be corrected, and objects within an image can be manipulated. This type of thing can be handled using conventional photographic techniques, but not without a great deal of difficulty. For many users the biggest advantage of the digital approach is the tremendous control that can be exercised over the colour balance of an image. A similar degree of control is probably available using conventional photographic printing techniques, but getting things just right can be a slow, difficult, and expensive business. Consequently, few photographers bother. Washed out sunsets remain washed out, unrealistic skin tones remain unrealistic, interior shots with strong orange colour casts stay that way, and so on.

The situation is very different with shots taken using a digital camera, or digital scans taken from photographic prints, negatives, or transparencies. Using a program such as Photoshop it is easy to remove even quite strong colour casts, sunsets can be as subtle or gaudy as you like, and skin tones can be perfect every time. Using the selection tools it is also possible to process certain parts of the image while leaving others unaltered. Problems such as "red-eye" can usually be corrected in a matter of seconds. In fact you have complete control over the colour balance of digital images.

Of course, you do not have to stick with the original colours at all. There is plenty of scope for being creative with colour. The same techniques that permit "red-eye" to be corrected also enable any object to be given a new colour. If you require an image that has blue roses and red bananas it is quite possible to do this using Photoshop. In fact any object in an image can be selected and turned to any desired colour.

Adjustments submenu

Most of the facilities required for adjusting colours are to be found in the Adjustments submenu, which is to be found under the Image menu (Figure 6.1). Some of these require little explanation, such as brightness and contrast, but others are a little more involved. Although most images can benefit from the facilities available in the Adjustments submenu, it is not a good idea to start altering things like colour balance and contrast just because they are there. You should resort to the Adjustments submenu because there is something wrong with the image that you wish to correct, or there is an enhancement you would like to make.

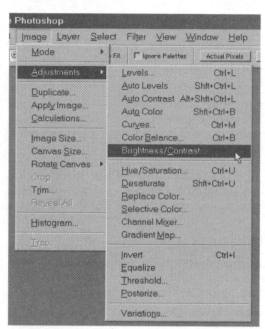

Fig.6.1 The Adjustments submenu

Fiddling with the settings for the sake of it is likely to make images worse rather than better.

Mode

If images are being produced for use on the web, simply use the default colour mode (RGB). The same is true for any application where the final output will be by way of a monitor, such as presentations stored on CD-ROMs. The CMYK mode is the obvious choice for images that will be output via professional equipment that uses this four-colour system. You should certainly switch to this mode before making any final adjustments to the colour balance, but many prefer to use the RGB mode initially.

Fig.6.2 The Variations screen offers lighter and darker versions plus six variations in colour balance

I suppose that the CMYK mode is also the obvious choice for images that will be output to your own inkjet printer. Bear in mind though, that these printers are not guaranteed to accurately produce the standard CMYK colour set. Consequently, there is little point in converting images to the CMYK mode, and the RGB mode can be used throughout. The printer and its driver software should convert the RGB image data to its own form of CMYK colour reproduction, giving good results.

Variations

Correcting colour imbalances by adjusting the primary colours is the obvious way of handling things, but this method is a skilled task. Photoshop provides easier ways of tackling the problem, and it is perhaps better to start with these. Figure 6.2 shows the Variations window, which is launched by selecting the Variations option at the bottom of the Adjustments submenu. The top section of the window shows the original image and the modified version, but these will be the same initially.

Fig.6.3 The original version of the image

The lower section of the window shows the modified image surrounded by six variations that have extra cyan, magenta, yellow, red, green, and blue. It is possible but unlikely that one of these variations will be exactly what is required. In that event, it is just a matter of left-clicking on the appropriate version, and the modified image will then adjust to match it. Operate the OK button to return to the image and make the changes take effect.

In most cases some extra processing will be required. The basic colour casts are quite weak, but by double clicking on one of the tinted images two or three times it is possible to obtain stronger effects. You can also double click on different images to combine two tints. Double clicking on the lighter and darker images in the right-hand section of the window respectively lightens or darkens the modified image by a small amount. Again, double clicking two or three times gives a stronger effect. In this way it is possible to gradually "fine tune" the image until it is exactly as required. Simply double click on the unmodified image to remove all the processing and start again. The OK button is operated when the desired effect is obtained, or the Cancel button is operated if you change your mind and wish to abandon the processing.

Fig.6.4 The highlights have been darkened and the shadows have been lightened

To the right of the Current Pick thumbnail there is a small slider control that can be used to increase or reduce the amount of change per mouse click. Each position it is moved to the right doubles the amount of change, and each position to the left halves the amount of change. It can be useful to move this control one or two positions to the left in order to correct minor colour casts, of for "fine tuning" larger changes. The changes tend to become quite large if it is moved to the right, but this can be useful for combating strong colour casts or adding special effects.

Shadows and highlights

The four radio buttons provide individual adjustment of the highlights, mid tones, shadows, and colour saturation. The mid tone option is used by default, and you might find that the desired correction can be obtained using this option. For best results the processing should be applied separately to the shadows, mid tones, and highlights. It is not possible to show the results of colour changes here, but Figure 6.3 shows the original image while Figure 6.4 shows one that has had the highlights darkened, and the shadows lightened. This has reduced the contrast of

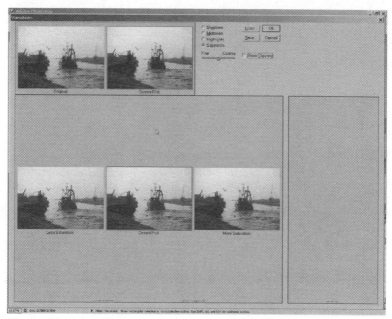

Fig.6.5 The simplified layout for adjusting saturation

the image, which shows that the Variations screen provides contrast control, even if it is via a slightly roundabout method.

The fourth radio button permits the colour saturation to be controlled, and the Variations window changes when this option is selected. The simplified layout of Figure 6.5 is provided, and this still has the original and current versions of the picture at the top. There are only three versions of the image in the lower part of the window though. These show the current image, a less saturated version, and a more saturated version. It is important not to confuse brightness and saturation. The overall brightness of the more saturated image is likely to be a little higher than that of the less saturated version, but this is not the main change.

Increasing the saturation produces stronger and purer colours. Reducing saturation gives weaker colours. In fact a greyscale image will be obtained if the saturation is reduced too far. In theory it is possible to make weak colours as strong as required by increasing the saturation, but with real-world images there can be problems. The usual problem is graininess or patterns appearing in what should be plain areas of the image. Figure

*Fig.6.6 The patterns in the sky are far more obvious in the colour
version of this image*

6.6 shows the type of thing that happens, but it is somewhat watered
down by the conversion to black and white. While high saturation levels
can produce some interesting and atmospheric effects, most of the time
this will probably not be what you are trying to achieve.

Clipping

There is a checkbox labelled Show Clipping. Clipping is where one or
more of the primary colours would be pushed beyond their maximum or
minimum values by the processing. Of course, the values would not
actually be taken beyond the normal limits. They would be set at the
maximum or minimum figures, as appropriate. The problem with clipping
is that light and dark areas tend to become enlarged, with no detail at all
in those areas. This will not necessarily matter, but in some instances it
will result in the loss of important details. Where only one or two of the
primary colours are clipped there will be a change in the colour balance
of the affected areas.

The areas that will be clipped are highlighted in inverse video if the Show
Clipping checkbox is ticked (Figure 6.7). For example, yellow is used if

Fig.6.7 Clipped areas can be highlighted in inverse video

blue will be clipped at full strength, and black is used if all the colours are clipped at minimum strength. This makes the clipped areas easy to spot and gives a good indication of the colours that are involved. Of course, clipping might not have any detrimental effects on the image, and as always it is the quality of the final image that counts. If a clipped image gives the result you require, then use it that way.

Load and Save

When the image is as required, simply operate the OK button to make the changes take effect. Use the Cancel button to exit the Variations window without making any changes. There are two more buttons, and these permit a set of adjustments to be saved or loaded. With image processing it is not uncommon for more or less the same processing to be applied to image after image. A digital camera or scanner might always produce the same colour cast with outdoor shots or consistently produce results that are slightly too dark.

Ideally this type of thing should be tackled at source, but a standard set of corrections can be applied via the Variations window where this is not practical. Start by loading an image into Photoshop and applying the required corrections using the Variations window in the normal way. Then operate the Save button, which produces the usual file browser (Figure 6.8). Choose a suitable filename for the set of corrections (e.g. cam_outdoors) and operate the Save button. To apply these settings to another image, load it into Photoshop and launch the Variations window. Operate the

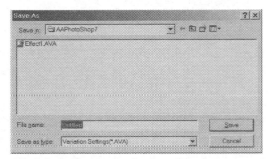

Fig.6.8 Saving a set of corrections for reuse with other images

Load button, select the correct file using the browser that appears, and then operate the Open button. The Current Pick image will change in response to the loaded changes, which can be applied to the image by operating the OK button.

The Variations window provides the easiest means of altering the colour balance and brightness of a picture. When it can provide the changes you need, the Variations window is probably the best method to use, particularly if you have little or no experience at editing images. Although it represents the easiest method, you will still have to try editing a few images in order to master the techniques. It is a good idea to master the basics of colour correction using this method before moving on to the alternatives provided by Photoshop.

Histogram

Although the Variations facility can handle the vast majority of colour correction, and it can also produce some special effects, many users eventually move on the more direct forms of control. These are perhaps more suitable for images that need large amounts of correction or where special effects are involved. It is only fair to point out that a picture having very serious colour or exposure problems is unlikely to produce top quality results however expertly it is processed. Using Photoshop it is

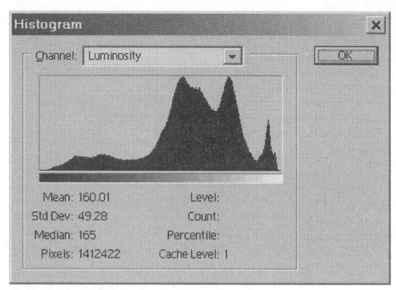

Fig.6.9 A histogram for the luminosity of an image

possible to make the most of the information in the image file, but it will not "make a silk purse out of a sow's ear".

The Histogram function in the Image menu is useful for showing the contrast and colour balance of an image. It only provides information about an image, and it is not possible to make changes via this function. Figure 6.9 shows the histogram produced for the picture of the artist painting the seascape. The bar immediately below the histogram shows a greyscale that goes from black on the left to white on the right. The height of the graph above each tone indicates the number of pixels that have that level of luminosity.

A well exposed picture would normally have a fair number of pixels from black right through to white. In this example a wide range or luminosity values are covered, but things fall away slightly at the dark end of the graph. The image is perhaps slightly on the light side, but there is clearly plenty of information available, and using Photoshop it should be possible to add a bit more "punch" to the picture.

Using the channel menu it is possible to show histograms for each of the (RGB) primary colours. Figure 6.10 shows the green channel histogram for the seascape image. It is worth looking at these individual histograms when a print has a very strong colour cast. If the mean value indicated in the statistics is very low or high for one of the colours it might not be possible to correct the colour imbalance convincingly. Always keep the nature of the picture in mind when looking at these histograms. Clearly a picture such as a close-up of a bright

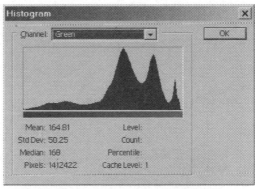

Fig.6.10 A histogram can be displayed for each channel

red flower will not have a nicely balanced colour content, and adjusting the image for such a balance will not give good results.

Figure 6.11 is a good example of the type of thing that you do not normally wish to see for either the luminosity or individual colours. This was produced from a scan of a rather pale print that lacked contrast. Although

the print is seriously overexposed, there are no true whites or even anything approaching a true white. With pictures of this type it is possible to boost the contrast so that it covers the full range, and the resultant picture might look quite good superficially. There is usually an obvious lack of detail though, and a massive

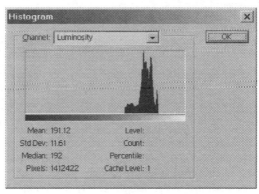

Fig.6.11 A histogram of this type indicates poor basic image quality

increase in contrast tends to produce rather grainy looking results. It is often better to settle for a limited boost in contrast with pictures that are well out of kilter. As always, it is ultimately the look of the image that counts and not its statistics.

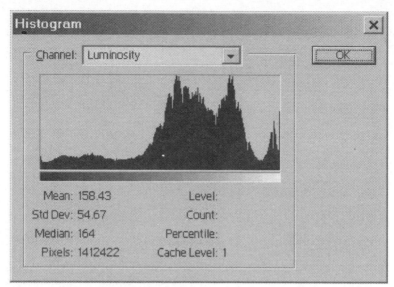

Fig.6.12 *Auto Levels gives a full contrast range, but will not necessarily give good colour balance*

Auto Levels

The Auto Levels option in the Adjustments submenu provides the quickest of fixes for problems with colour balance, brightness, and contrast. Photoshop examines the data in the image file and adjusts it to produce 100 percent contrast and what it "thinks" will be the best colour balance. This instant fix often works well when applied to images that are only fractionally below par. Figure 6.12 shows the histogram that resulted from using the Auto Levels function with the seascape image. The contrast has been boosted slightly and there are now significant numbers of pixels at both extremes of the range. The amount of blue in the picture was also boosted slightly, giving a more plausible look to the sea and sky. Although the changes were quite small, they produced a definite improvement in the image quality. An improvement in results will not always be produced though.

It can be useful to try the Auto Levels function with images that are obviously lacking in contrast, are overexposed, or are underexposed. The results might be good, or sufficiently good that only a small amount of manual adjustment is needed in order to get the pictures just right. It only takes a click of the mouse to undo the processing in cases where it

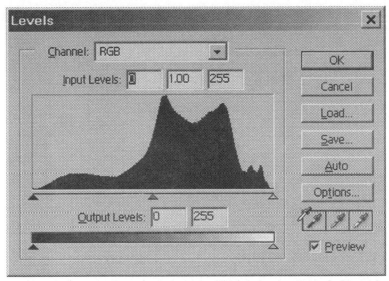

Fig.6.13 The Levels windows provides a histogram and some controls

has totally missed the mark.   Even if you do not use the settings it produces, Auto Levels enables you to see the effect of pushing the image to 100 percent contrast.   If the boost in contrast produces obvious problems, then you know that a more restrained approach is needed. Note that not all images are at their best with 100 percent contrast. With some images of flowers for example, there can be large colour contrasts but relatively little contrast in terms of luminosity. Pushing the contrast to its limits can produce odd effects with images of this type, such as flowers or other objects that seem to glow from within. Patterns and textures can become grossly exaggerated.

Levels

As can be seen from Figure 6.13, choosing Levels from the Adjustments submenu produces a window that includes a histogram. However, in this case the window is a dialogue box that does include controls that permit the contrast and brightness of the image to be altered. There are two sets of slider controls, and the lower set controls the maximum and minimum luminosity. Dark grey can be set as the minimum level instead of black by moving the left-hand slider to the right. Similarly, light grey

Fig.6.14 The original version of the Pelicans photograph

rather than white can be set as the maximum level by moving the right-hand slider to the left. Reductions in contrast of this type are not often needed, but some subjects can benefit from this treatment. Some printing processes require a reduction in contrast of this type to prevent large dark areas from printing as solid areas of black.

The upper set of sliders is of greater use to most users. If the slider at the white end is moved inwards, areas that were previously light grey become white, and the lower levels of luminosity are shuffled upwards. Adjusting the slider at the other end produces a similar effect with dark greys becoming black and higher levels of luminosity being shuffled downwards. Neither type of adjustment is normally applied to a picture that already has a full range of tones. Doing so would result in clipping. The idea is to move the sliders inwards so that they match the lightest and darkest tones present in the image, as indicated by the histogram. This gives the full contrast range from the image.

Figure 6.14 shows a photograph of the Pelicans in St. James Park drying their feathers after an early morning shower. It is somewhat lacking in sparkle, and the histogram shows a lack of highlights plus dark tones

Fig.6.15 The image has been adjusted for a full contrast range

that are something less than black. Moving the two sliders inwards to match up with the lightest and darkest tones present in the image has given much better contrast without producing any clipping (Figure 6.15). Note that it is best to have the Preview checkbox ticked so that the effect of changes to the controls can be seen on the image. The effect on contrast is much the same as when using Auto Levels function, but when the levels are adjusted manually it is possible to set less than the full contrast range.

The upper set of slider controls includes an additional control in the middle. This is a very useful tool that should not be overlooked. It can be used to bring out details that are tending to disappear in dark areas of the image. I often photograph small objects that are being sold on Internet auction sites, and a lack of detail in dark areas is a common problem with this type of thing. Figure 6.16 shows a photograph of a bright red jewel box, and although the photograph has a full range of tones, the box is rather dark. It looks somewhat worse in colour than it does in Figure 6.16. A general increase in brightness would lighten the box, but light areas of the picture would be clipped.

Fig.6.16 This image has a full range of tones but the box looks too dark

Better results are obtained by moving the middle slider control to the left. The tone selected using this control becomes the new mid-tone, and the others are moved upward to accommodate this change. This brightens the darker areas of the picture (Figure 6.17), but it does not cause significant clipping. The middle slider control can be used to combat the opposite problem where a picture that has the full contrast range is too bright. Moving the middle control to the right produces a general downward shift in the brightness of the picture, but with minimal clipping.

Eyedropper

The Levels function can be used in an automatic mode where the colour balance as well as the brightness is adjusted. The automatic operation is achieved with the aid of the Eyedropper tool. The basic idea is to indicate a point on the image that should be black, white, or a mid-grey

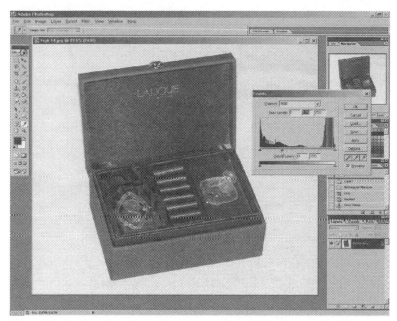

Fig.6.17 The box has been lightened without clipping the highlights

colour. Photoshop then automatically adjusts the colour balance and brightness of the image so that the selected spot is the right colour, and this should remove the colour cast from the image. This method is not totally reliable in practice, since it is dependent on the user finding a spot on the image that should be pure black or white, or a neutral grey at a mid-tone. Finding a suitable grey is quite difficult, and there may not be a suitable colour on the image.

Most images have something very close to pure black or white, or what would be pure black or white if there was no colour cast, and using one of these is a more practical option. However, an area that looks as though it should be black or white may actually have slight coloration. This colour will be removed by the processing, and the whole image will be given the same treatment. The colour cast will not be accurately counteracted, and a new colour cast will be introduced. Another potential problem is that what appears to be black might actually be dark grey, and an apparently white area might be very pale grey. This can result in unacceptable lightening or darkening of the image. Of course, if things do not go perfectly the first time, the processing can be removed and another spot on the image can be used as the reference point. Sometimes this method works, but with some images there are no suitable reference colours.

Near the bottom right-hand corner of the Levels window there are three eyedropper tools available, and from left to right these are used with black, mid-grey, and white levels. To apply colour correction the appropriate eyedropper button is selected and then a suitable point on the image is selected using the eyedropper tool. In my experience this method of colour correction usually works best using the black as the reference colour. Therefore, I use the black eyedropper tool first and then the white one if the initial attempts are unsuccessful. With most images it is possible to find a good black level to use as the reference, and the colour cast is then instantly removed.

Even if the correction is not perfect, this method will usually get quite close to the correct colour balance, and some "fine tuning" can then be applied using another method. It is much easier than applying all the colour correction "by eye".

The channel menu enables the individual primary colours to be selected and processed separately. Presumably it would be possible to automatically adjust the balance of each channel using mid-tone primary colours as references, but these will not be present in most images.

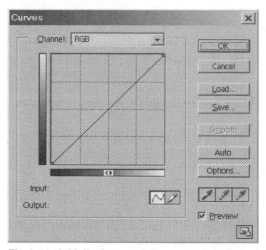

Adjusting the settings for each channel permits the colour balance to be adjusted manually, but this is not the only way of manually adjusting the colour balance.

Curves

The Curves facility has similar features to the Levels facility, but it is even more versatile. The Levels dialogue box has single slider for

Fig.6.18 Initially the graph has a straight line and no curves

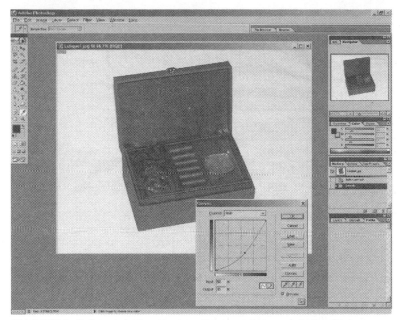

Fig.6.19(a) A downward curve produces an increase in brightness

controlling mid tones, but the Curves window effectively provides numerous controls that can be used to mould the contrast and brightness precisely as required. When the Curves window is opened there is a noticeable lack of curves. Instead, there is a graph that has a straight line going from the bottom left-hand corner to the top right-hand corner (Figure 6.18). What is the graph showing? It simply shows the input levels on the horizontal scale versus the output levels on the vertical scale.

As things stand, each input level produces an identical output level, and no processing is applied. The line can be dragged into a curve, as in Figure 6.19(a), and this alters the relationship between the input and output values. The zero and 100 percent input levels still produce zero and 100 percent output levels, but changes occur at other levels. The readout near the bottom left-hand corner of the window shows that there is a 58 percent input level and a 35 percent output level at the point where the line was dragged. Lower values give higher brightness, so dragging the line in this direction produces an increase in brightness

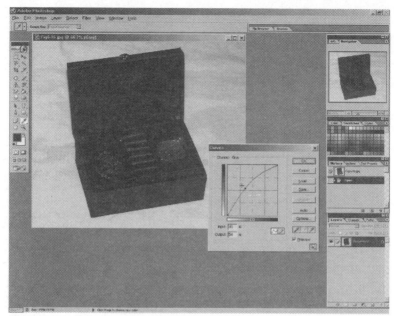

Fig.6.19(b) Dragging the curve in the opposite direction gives a reduction in the overall brightness

without introducing significant clipping. Dragging the line in the opposite direction, as in Figure 6.19(b) gives a reduction in brightness.

In Figures 19(a) and 19(b) low values represent high luminosity values. This is indicated by the two greyscale bars, which have the white ends in the bottom left-hand corner. Left-clicking on the horizontal greyscale bar switches things around the other way, with low values giving low levels of luminosity. An upward curve then gives increased brightness, and a downward curve gives reduced brightness. Use whichever setting you find the easier to work with. The descriptions provided here assume that low values give high brightness.

It is possible to obtain input and output values for any point on the line by first moving the pointer away from the line so that an ordinary arrow pointer is obtained. Then hold down the left mouse button and move the pointer along the line. The readout will show the input and output levels for the current position of the pointer, and it will automatically update as the pointer is moved. Just place the pointer anywhere on the line while still holding down the left mouse button and the readout will show the corresponding input and output levels.

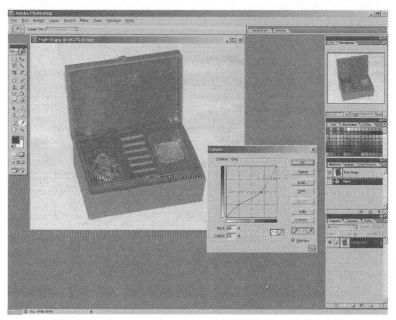

Fig.6.20 There can be more than one control point on the curve

Using one point on the graph line gives a little more control than the Levels method, but not much. Greater control can be obtained by dragging other points on the line, which gives more control points. Suppose that you needed to make the jewel box photograph lighter, but without making the background any lighter than it is already. First a point is placed on the line at about the 25 percent input/output level. This is done to effectively anchor the lower part of the line in place so that it is not influenced by adjustments made higher up. With the first point in place the upper part of the line is then dragged downward (Figure 6.20). The darker parts of the picture have been lightened, but there is no change to the bright background or other parts of the photograph that have similar luminance levels.

It is possible to have up to 16 points on the line, which effectively provide separate brightness controls for various bands of luminance values. Odd effects can be obtained by using complex curves, as in the example of Figure 6.21. In most cases two or three control points and some fairly simple curves are all that will be needed.

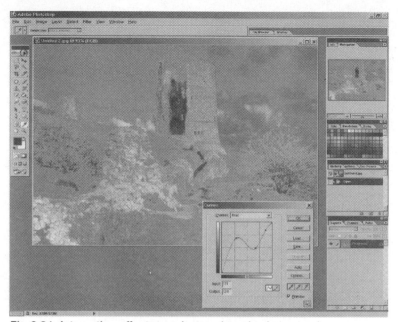

Fig.6.21 Interesting effects can be produced using complex curves

Dragging the bottom of the line upwards reduces the maximum level to a shade of grey rather than white. Moving the top of the line downwards gives a shade of grey instead of white as the minimum level. This is the same as adjusting the lower set of slider controls in the Levels window, and it reduces contrast (Figure 6.22). Moving the top and bottom of the line inwards, as in Figure 6.23, is equivalent to using the upper set of slider controls in the Levels window, and it increases contrast. However, there is no histogram in the Curves window to assist this type of adjustment. Unless you prefer to make this type of adjustment purely "by eye" it is better to use the Levels window.

Like the Levels window, the Curves window includes a Channel menu that permits each primary colour to be adjusted separately. This gives tremendous control over the colour balance, but it not exactly an easy way of adjusting the colours. It is probably of more use for special effects than it is for everyday adjustments of colour balance. There are two buttons below the graph, and the one on the left is used by default. The button on the right gives an alternative method of controlling the graph line. The line can be drawn onto the graph when this freehand mode is

Fig.6.22 The contrast can be reduced using the Curves window

Fig.6.23 Producing an increase in contrast is equally straightforward

used. It is not necessary to draw a complete line, and Photoshop will merge the section you draw with the existing line.

Brightness/Contrast

This option produces the small window shown in Figure 6.24. The two slider controls are conventional contrast and brightness controls, much

*Fig.6.24 Conventional brightness
and contrast controls
are available*

like those fitted to television sets and computer monitors. While these clearly represent the easiest way of adjusting the brightness and (or) contrast of an image, they also provide a relatively limited amount of control. I do not mean limited in the sense that only a small range of brightness and contrast levels are available. In this sense there is a massive

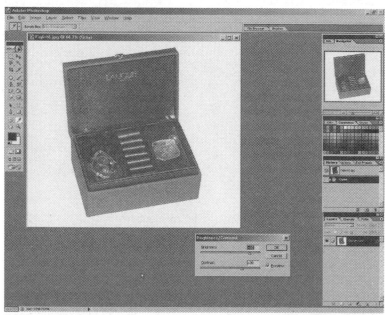

Fig.6.25 The box has been lightened, but there are clipped highlights

amount of control available. It is subtlety that is lacking with this method of control. One of the other methods is needed if you find yourself moving the controls this way and that, unable to find satisfactory settings.

The brightness control simply moves all the colour values up or down by a certain amount. The contrast control produces a wider spread of values. In both cases severe clipping will occur if the controls are not adjusted with due care. In Figure 6.25 the photograph of the jewel box has been adjusted using the Brightness and Contrast controls, and plenty of detail can be seen in the previously dark areas of the box. First the brightness was increased in order lighten the overly dark areas. Then the contrast was boosted in order to counteract the perceived loss of contrast produced by increasing the brightness.

This processing has brought out the details in the box, but the background has changed from pale yellow to pure white due to the clipping that has occurred. The highlights in the box have suffered a similar fate. The image lacks "punch", but setting the contrast any higher will increase the clipping problem.

It is clear from the histogram of the adjusted image (Figure 6.26) that all is not well. Most of the pixels are in a fairly narrow range of mid tones, with the rest at the white end of the tone range. The Brightness and Contrast controls are the obvious tools for adjusting their respective aspects of an image, but in

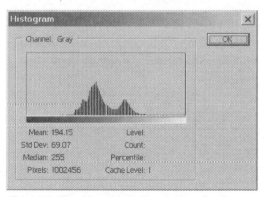

Fig.6.26 The histogram shows the clipping and lack of contrast

practice they are unlikely to provide the best results. Setting a good contrast range and then adjusting the mid tones using the Levels or Curves window gives much better results with awkward images.

Note that the brightness and contrast can be controlled by typing values into the two textboxes. Both cover a range of values from –100 to +100. In general it is easier to use the sliders and the preview facility to adjust the brightness and contrast by "eye". The textboxes could be useful if you need to apply standard corrections to images.

Fig.6.27 The original image lacks contrast

Auto Contrast

The Auto Levels feature was mentioned previously, but there are a couple of alternative quick fix options. These effectively split the colour and contrast correction facilities of the Auto Levels feature into two separate options. The Auto Contrast option provides an instant means of adjusting an image for a full range of tones. Figure 6.27 shows a scanned image of a nuthatch climbing a tree trunk, and there is a noticeable lack of contrast. The bright sky breaking through the gaps in the branches is not that bright, and the dark areas of the bark are far from black.

An image such as this will usually look at its best with 100 percent contrast, making it a good candidate for automatic adjustment. The effect of the Auto Contrast function can be seen from Figure 6.28. If necessary the Auto Contrast function can be followed by some manual adjustment of the mid tones using the Levels function, to get the overall brightness correct. This combination represents the quickest and easiest approach where a full range of tones is required.

Fig.6.28 The Auto Contrast facility has produced a full range of tones

There is also an Auto Color option available for colour images. This is not something that could be regarded as one of Photoshop's most useful features. There is no harm in trying this feature, since it can be undone using the History palette or the Undo facility. Photoshop does not know whether the image is a seascape or a bunch of flowers, so an automatic colour balance facility inevitably involves some technical guesswork. Sometimes it will be right or quite close, but often the results will be a long way out.

Color Balance

The Color Balance window (Figure 6.29) enables the colour balance to be adjusted via three slider controls. This can look a little confusing at first, with the RGB primary colours at one end of the scale and CMYK primary colours at the other. It is based on the standard artists' colour wheel, which uses an arrangement like the one shown in Figure 6.30. A proper colour wheel would actually have numerous segments of colour, or even a continuous change from one primary colour to the next. The

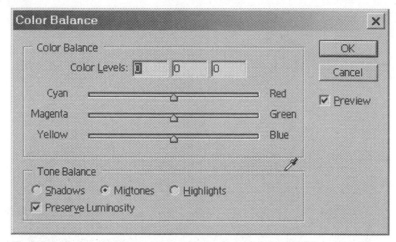

Fig.6.29 The colour balance is adjusted via the three slider controls

colour bars in the Photoshop Color palette and Color Picker are effectively linear versions of the colour wheel.

Colour wheels are of importance to artists because they show the complementary colour for every colour of the spectrum. Many artists produce dark colours by mixing them with a complementary colour rather than with black or a dark grey. The colour wheel shows complementary colours on opposite sides of the wheel (blue and yellow for example), making it easier to find accurate complements for any hue. The three slider controls in the Color Balance window form a sort of highly simplified colour wheel, having only the primary colours. If the top slider control is moved to the right you are either adding more red or reducing the amount of cyan, depending on how you look at things.

In order to make corrections to the colour balance using this method it is important to have a good eye for colour. It is advisable to get the contrast and brightness set correctly before moving on to the colour balance. Make sure that the Preserve Luminosity check box is ticked so that changes to the colour settings will not alter the brightness and contrast. Of course, also have the Preview checkbox ticked so that you can immediately see the results when the sliders are adjusted.

Before making any adjustments, look at the image and decide what colour needs to be altered. The colour cast might be something simple such as too much yellow, and moving the yellow/blue slider to produce more

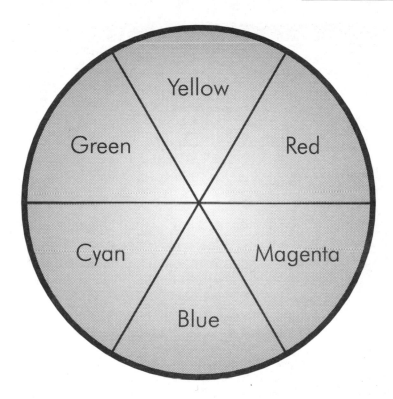

Fig.6.30 The general arrangement used in a standard colour wheel

blue should correct the problem. In most cases it will be necessary to adjust two or three of the sliders in order to obtain the desired result. For example, photographs taken indoors using tungsten lighting tend to have a strong orange cast, and normally require a reduction in the red and yellow levels. It is as well to try adjusting the third slider as well, as this might give slightly improved colour balance.

Experience is important with this type of thing, so it is more than a little helpful to load a variety of images into Photoshop and experiment with the colour balance controls until you are familiar with their operation. While it is desirable to get the colour balance as accurate as possible, do not fall into the trap of spending large amounts of time making fine adjustments that never seem to get the colour absolutely perfect. If the colour balance looks about right, then it is good enough.

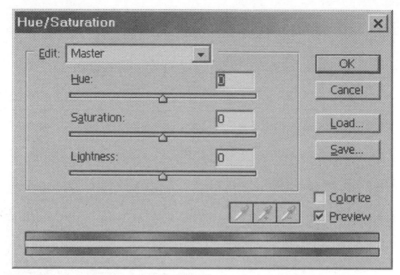

Fig.6.31 The Hue/Saturation window also has a Lightness control

Also bear in mind that you are allowed a bit of artistic licence. The photograph of the pelicans in the park was taken in the early morning, and there was consequently a slight red bias in the picture. Instead of removing the red bias it was exaggerated slightly in the final print to give a slightly more obvious early morning feel to the picture. It is not a good idea to get carried away with this type of thing, but giving the colours a little help will often enhance the atmosphere of a picture.

Strong colour casts might be beyond the adjustment range of the Color Balance controls. The simple solution is to set as much correction as possible initially, and then operate the OK button to make the changes take effect. Then go back into the Color Balance window and add further correction. This process can be repeated again if necessary, but bear in mind that the chances of correcting really strong colour casts are not good. The weak colour or colours will often be so weak that they can not be boosted to full strength without odd effects occurring.

Hue/Saturation

The name of this option suggests that there are two controls, but the Hue/Saturation window actually has three slider controls (Figure 6.31). In addition to controls for hue and colour there is also a Lightness control.

The Edit menu near the top of the window enables the individual colours or the full range via the default Master option. Use the Master setting when making initial experiments with the Hue/Saturation facility. As with the other colour/brightness adjustment windows, the Preview checkbox should be ticked so that changes can be viewed on the image.

I think it is fair to say that the Hue control is a bit confusing. If you try experimenting with various settings it will probably appear to be producing random colour changes. The two colour bars at the bottom of the window were not placed there to make it look pretty, and if you move the Hue control to the right the lower colour bar will shift to the left. Although it is only a greyscale image, the shift can be seen in Figure 6.32 (compare this to Figure 6.31). Move the Hue control to the left, and the lower colour bar moves to the right.

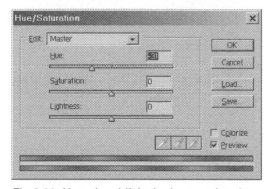

What the two colour bars are showing are the input and output colours. With the Hue control at a central setting the two bars are aligned and the

Fig.6.32 Note the shift in the lower colour bar

input colour is always the same as the output colour. Move the control slightly to the left and yellow on the top bar (the input colour) is vertically aligned with orange on the lower bar (the output colour). There is a similar shift right across the spectrum. Move the Hue control slightly to the right and things are reversed, with orange being replaced with yellow, etc.

These small adjustments give what artists term warmer colours if the Hue control is moved to the left or colder colours if it is moved to the right. In other words, more red and more blue respectively. I find this is useful for adjusting skin tones. Skin tones that are too red giving a "lobster" effect can be corrected by moving the Hue control to the right. Slightly green and unnatural skin tones can usually be corrected by moving the Hue control fractionally to the left. More than slight changes produce massive colour shifts, and you are then into the realm of special effects.

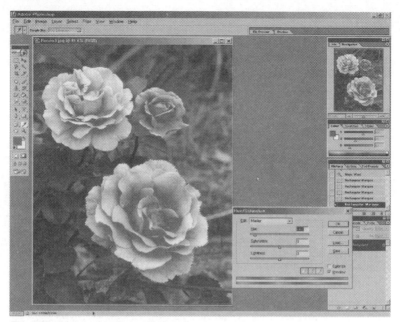

Fig.6.33 Using this large shift in hue turns the rose blue

So far it has been assumed that colour and brightness changes will be applied to the entire image. All the colour and brightness controls can be used with selections though, and the Hue control works particularly well with single objects or small groups. Try something like the set-up of Figure 6.33 where the largest rose in the improved rose photograph has been selected. Use any object that is easily selected, but try to choose something that is predominantly one colour such as a car, or the hull of boat. Then launch the Hue/Saturation window and try adjusting the Hue control. You should find that the object can be set at any colour of the spectrum. The rose in Figure 6.33 was originally salmon pink with a hint of yellow. The Hue setting shown in Figure 6.33 has turned it into that great rarity, the blue rose.

"Red-eye" removal

An obvious application for this type of editing is the removal of the "red-eye" problem, which often occurs when photographing people using a flashgun built into or fitted on the camera. An easy way of selecting the offending areas of red is to first draw a rectangular marquee around them. Then set the Magic wand tool to the Insect mode and remove the tick from the Contiguous checkbox. With a fairly high tolerance value set, left-clicking on one eye should select both "red-eye" areas without selecting anything else.

It is then a matter of using the Hue and Saturation facility to change the red to the required colour. Browns for example, can be produced using orange as the hue, and then reducing the brightness. A small reduction in the saturation setting is usually needed as well. This control is described in the next section. With careful adjustment of the three controls it should be possible to set any desired colour.

Saturation

The Saturation control gives reduced colour saturation if it is moved to the left, and will leave a greyscale image if it is taken right to the end of the control range. Reducing saturation is helpful with an image that has excessively vivid colours, or it can be used to produce weak colours for special effect. Moving the saturation control to the right gives stronger colours, and weak colours can be corrected in this way. Many older scanners produce slightly weak colours and will benefit from a small boost in saturation. Resist the temptation to overdo the saturation and produce images that have "Mickey Mouse" colours.

The Lightness control is a standard brightness type that requires no further explanation. Incidentally, the lower colour bar changes in response to adjustments of the Saturation and Lightness controls, and not just the Hue type. You can therefore see the full range of colours available for the current lightness and saturation settings. This is clearly useful, but it is better to judge the effect by the image rather than the colours in the lower colour bar.

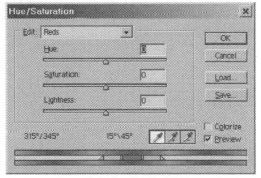

Fig.6.34 The Hue/Saturation window set for single colour operation

Single colour

Selecting a single colour from the Edit menu changes the window slightly (Figure 6.34). Sliders appear on the colour bars to indicate the colour range that will be altered by the Hue, Saturation, and Colour controls. There are two sets of sliders, with the inner pair indicating the range of colours that will be fully altered by adjustments to the controls. The outer pair indicates the colours that will be affected to a lesser extent.

With something like the roses photograph it is possible to alter their colour by adjusting the sliders to match the colours in the roses. Operating the Hue control then provides the colour shift. This type of thing does not work well with all photographs, since there will sometimes be other objects of a similar colour in the image. Where applicable, this method is usually much quicker and easier than using normal selection methods. Of course, it can be combined with normal selection methods. Remember that it is not just selective colour changes that can be implemented in this way. The lightness and saturation can also be limited to a particular colour range.

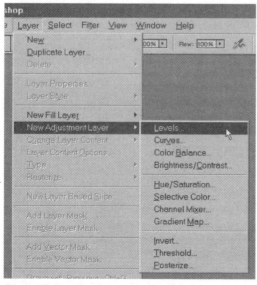

Fig.6.35 Creating a new adjustment layer

Adjustment layers

An adjustment layer is a special type of layer that contains adjustment details for the image on a lower layer. A set of adjustments is all that an adjustment layer can contain, and you can not paint or draw on this type of layer. An adjustment layer can be added by selecting New Adjustment Layer from the Layer menu, and then the required type of adjustment from the submenu

(Figure 6.35). The options available here are essentially the same as the ones in the Adjustments submenu. There is also a button at the bottom of the Layers palette that enables a new gradient or

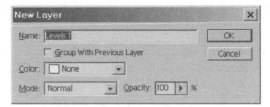

Fig.6.36 The New Layer window

adjustment layer to be produced. Either way, the small dialogue box of Figure 6.36 will appear. A few parameters can be changed here, but for most purposes the default settings will suffice.

Having created the layer, the appropriate control dialogue box will appear, which is the Levels type in the example of Figure 6.37. Notice also, that the new layer is now included in the Layers palette near the bottom right-hand corner of the screen. Adjustments to the controls will be applied to

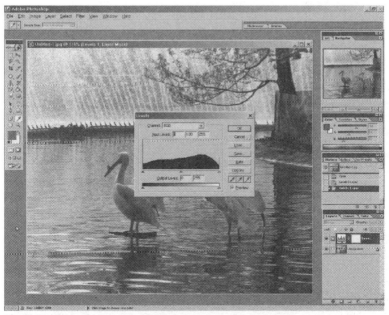

Fig.6.37 The appropriate dialogue box for the new layer will appear

6 Colour balance

Fig.6.38 The adjustment layer has been used to reduce the contrast

Fig.6.39 Deleting the adjustment layer removes the processing

Fig.6.40 The image has been "flattened" and the reduction in contrast has been retained

the image in the normal way, and in Figure 6.38 for example, the contrast has been greatly reduced.   In Figure 6.38 the changes have been accepted by operating the OK button, and they have been applied to the image in the normal way.

If you change your mind and wish to revert to the original version of the image it is just a matter of deleting the adjustment layer (Figure 6.39). The adjustment layer can be deleted by making it the current layer and then selecting Delete from the Layer menu, followed by Layer from the submenu that appears. Alternatively, drag its entry in the Layers palette to the trashcan icon in the bottom left-hand corner of the palette. The image can be merged into a single layer if you wish to make the changes permanent. Select Flatten from the Layers menu. The changes will be retained but the adjustment layer will be deleted (Figure 6.40). Note that the image will automatically be flattened if it is saved in a format that does not support adjustment layers, such as Jpeg. Save the image in Photoshop's PSD format if you wish to retain adjustment layers.

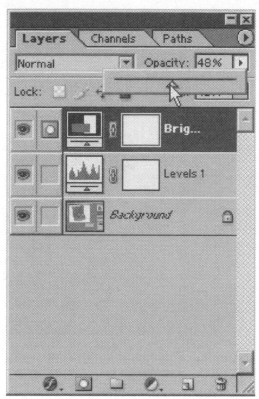

Fig.6.41 The Layers palette has an Opacity control, which can reduce the effect of an adjustment layer

More than one type of control can be implemented by adjustment layers, but a different layer must be used for each type of control. You can use one for adjusting colour balance and another for setting the brightness and contrast, for example. The Layers palette provides an Opacity control in the top right-hand corner (Figure 6.41). This may seem to have no relevance to an adjustment layer, but it permits the changes provided by the layer to be reduced. For example, if the layer provides increased contrast, reducing the opacity setting reduces the boost in contrast. At zero percent opacity the changes are removed completely.

Points to remember

A huge range of settings can be altered via the Adjustments submenu. Problems with colour balance, contrast, and brightness can all be handled via this submenu, and there are various means of combating these problems.

The Variations window provides an easy means of adjusting the colour balance and brightness. This is probably the best place for beginners to start, and it might be all you require. However, most users will wish to move on to more direct methods of control.

The Histogram facility shows the range of tones covered by the image, but it provides no means of adjusting them. The Levels facility provides a histogram and does include controls for contrast and brightness. These controls make it easy to set a suitable contrast range, and the overall brightness can be altered without introducing clipping.

The Curves facility offers similar facilities to the Levels type, but it provides greater control over the input/output transfer characteristic. This permits details to be brought out in dark areas without altering middle and light tones, and special effects can also be produced.

Small adjustments to the Hue control in the Hue and Saturation dialogue box are useful for making "cold" skin tones "warmer" and vice versa. Large changes produce totally different colours, which can be great for special effects. More normally, this facility is used selectively to produce a colour change, such as in "red-eye" removal.

Remember that some colour casts are not faults, but merely reflect the conditions when the photograph was taken. In some cases it can be better to increase the colour bias slightly rather than remove it. Provided it is not overdone, this method can be used to give a photograph more atmosphere.

Ordinary brightness and contrast controls are available. Care has to be taken when using these as it is easy to produce clipping, which loses details in light and (or) dark areas of the picture. The Levels and Curves facilities are much better for controlling brightness and contrast.

Reducing the colour saturation is useful for atmospheric effects, and can produce a sort of "watercolour" look to an image. Colour saturation can be increased where an image has weak colours, but it is best to be conservative. It is easy to produce unrealistically bright results, and there can be unwanted side effects when the saturation is boosted.

Adjustments can be applied to an image via an adjustment layer or layers. Deleting a layer removes the adjustments it applied, or merging it with the image applies them in the normal fashion.

Brush tools

Limitations

Photoshop is a versatile piece of software that can be used as a paint program, where images are produced from scratch and painted using the various brush tools that are available. As the first part of its name implies though, this is not really its primary purpose. Photoshop is actually quite potent as a paint program, but this is definitely not what brought it to prominence, or should that be dominance? Photoshop dominates

Fig.7.1 A photograph such as this provides an easy starting point

Fig.7.2 The object in the lake is to be retouched

the world of digital retouching, where you can simply paint out bits of photographs that you do not like, repair damage in old prints, and so on. Retouching photographs is not exactly new, and it has probably been around for almost as long as there have been photographs. However, it is much easier to achieve good results using the digital version, and the range of possibilities is larger.

With conventional retouching the photograph is altered using special paints and inks. These can be applied using conventional brushes or an airbrush. The direct equivalent of this with Photoshop is to mix the desired colours and then paint them onto the image using the various brush tools. The trouble with this approach is that photographs do not usually have large areas of one colour. There are usually colour graduations and plain areas usually have more texture than is apparent at first glance. A lack of graduations and texture can make the retouched areas stand out like the proverbial "sore thumb". The simple painting approach can work well with small areas, but it takes a lot of effort and skill to produce the textures to make larger areas look convincing.

Fig.7.3 The Brush menu can be greatly enlarged if required

Fig.7.4 Some example brushstrokes

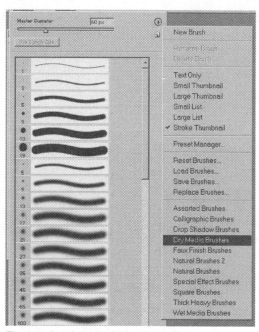

Fig.7.5 A submenu is available from the Brush menu

The photograph of the pelicans in the park (Figure 7.1) provides a good example of a photograph that is easily retouched using any of the normal techniques. Make your initial experiments with something fairly straightforward such as this. The obvious problem with this photograph is the bits of what I presume are either water pipes or twigs that are sticking up out of the lake. These slightly spoil the tranquil scene and are an unwanted distraction. We will start with the object sticking up out the water between the two pelicans. Zooming in on the relevant part of the picture (Figure 7.2) shows that the water around the object is produced by a pattern of short horizontal lines. The colours are various greys and browns reflected from the trees and sky in the background.

Painting over this type of thing is very easy. It is made easier by the fact that the resolution of the photograph is not very high, and the individual pixels are clearly visible even using a modest amount of zoom. In general, the higher the resolution of an image the more carefully it has to be retouched. The lines that depict the water are mostly just one pixel high, and a very small brush size is needed in order to paint similar lines over the unwanted object. Brush size is often important with retouching work, but all the more so with the simple painting technique.

A wide range of preset brush styles and sizes are available from the Brush menu in the Options bar (Figure 7.3). This becomes available in the Options bar when any brush or brush type tool is selected. The default size of this menu is quite small, but it can be dragged to a larger size via the triangle in the bottom right-hand corner. Having a larger range of brushes displayed avoids excessive scrolling of the options. Figure 7.4 shows some lines drawn using a few of the brushes from this menu. As will be apparent from this, more than just simple brushes of various widths are available. Some of the brushes produce special effects.

Brush width

It is a good idea to produce a blank page using the New option from the File menu and then try some of the brushes. Note that the width of any brush can be altered via the slider control near the top of the Brush menu. A submenu can be produced by left-clicking the small button in the top right-hand corner of the menu (Figure 7.5). Some of the options alter the way the menu is presented, such as giving a text only version, but most users prefer the default style. Alternative brush sets are available, and loading one of these results in the menu changing to suit new brushes.

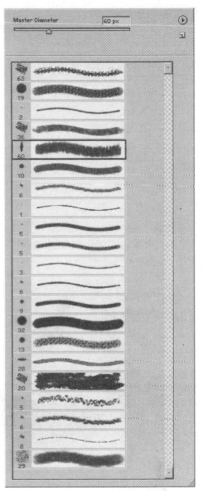

Fig.7.6 The Dry Media menu

Figure 7.6 shows the menu with the Dry Media Brushes loaded. These mimic pencils, charcoal, pastels, etc.

The Brushes palette (Figure 7.7) is also available, and can be launched by operating the Brushes tab to the right of the Options bar, or selecting Brushes from the Window menu. This palette enables custom brushes

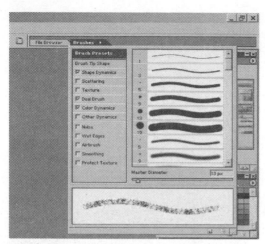

Fig.7.7 The Brushes palette is similar to the Brush menu

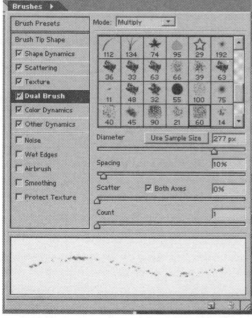

Fig.7.8 Various control panels are available

to be produced, and various control panels are available by selecting options from the list down the left-hand side of the window. One of these is shown in Figure 7.8. The panel at the bottom of the palette gives a preview of the effect that the selected brush design will produce.

It is worth taking some time to experiment with the preset brush sets and the options available from the Brushes palette. However, the brushes in the default set are perfectly adequate for most photographic retouching work. The default brushes are divided into three main groups, and one of these is the type that produces well defined lines with "clean" edges. The largest group produce simple lines but with fuzzy edges. The third group produce textures and effects. The brushes with blurred edges are good for retouching images, as the fuzzy edges often help

Fig.7.9 There it is, gone!

blend the newly added material with the original image. In this example
the retouching is being done on a pixel by pixel basis, and a standard
(non-fuzzy) brush with a width of one pixel is probably the best choice.

Cloning

Figure 7.9 shows a close-up of the retouched part of the image, and
Figure 7.10 shows the full image, minus the offending object. To
demonstrate that it can be done, I did things the hard way and mixed
colours that fitted in well with those already on the screen, painting a few
lines with each colour. In most cases it is much easier and better to
select suitable colours from the image using the Eyedropper tool. Even
if your "eye" for colour is not very good, this method should ensure that
the retouching blends in well with the rest of the image.

Fig.7.10 The full photograph with the object removed

There is an even easier way, which is to use the Clone tool instead of the ordinary Brush tool. Using the Clone tool it is possible to copy material from one part of an image to another. The Clone tool can live up to its name and produce duplicate objects in an image. In Figure 7.11 half a dozen boats, complete with shadows, have been added to the picture. The Clone tool often provides a quick and easy way of handling this type of thing, but it does not necessarily provide the best approach.

There can be perspective problems, and the additional white dinghy near the bottom right-hand corner of the image demonstrates this. It appears larger and a slightly different shape to the original, which is the one nearer the corner. It is actually identical to the original, and it is perceived as larger as it is further from the viewpoint, and should therefore be smaller. Also, it should be foreshortened slightly as it is further away and being viewed at a less steep angle. This makes it look slightly longer than the original. These problems can be counteracted if an object is selected and then cloned using the Copy and Paste facilities. The scaling

Fig.7.11 The Clone tool has been used to add half a dozen boats to this image

and distorting facilities can be used to give more convincing results. These are not available when using the Clone tool.

Cover-up

The Clone tool excels at painting over unwanted objects or blemishes by copying from surrounding areas. This method has been used to remove the unwanted object in the version of the pelican image shown in Figure 7.12. In Figure 7.13 it has additionally been used to remove the pipes towards the left-hand side of the image. It has also been used to remove what I think is probably a branch sticking up out of the lake under the right wing of the pelican on the right-hand side. We are all familiar with the problem of trees in the background seeming to grow

Fig.7.12 The object was easily removed using the Clone tool

out of the heads of people in the foreground. This type of problem can actually occur with all sorts of photographs, and in the original colour version of this photograph the impression was very much that there was a strange growth coming out of the pelican's wing!

Painting using the Cloning tool is similar to using the ordinary Brush tool, but there are some important differences. As normal, a suitable brush has to be selected. Filling large areas is quicker using a large brush, but a small brush is often needed for filling in fine detail. Accordingly, it is often a matter of starting with a large brush and moving down to a small one for the final touches. In this case only small areas are involved, so a fine brush having a width of a few pixels is all that is required. With a normal brush you "paint" on the screen by dragging the brush. In other words, you hold down the left mouse button while moving the mouse.

The same method is used with the Clone tool, but an error message will be produced if you try to use it without first indicating what you wish to clone. You do this by first placing the pointer at the centre of the material

Fig.7.13 The final image with all the unwanted objects removed

you wish to clone and pressing the Alt key. Incidentally, when using any form of brush tool the pointer is actually an outline of the brush. You can therefore see the exact size and shape of the selected brush. When you press the Alt key, the pointer will change to a sort of crosshairs sight. Drag the pointer to the centre of the area that will be retouched, release the left mouse button, and then release the Alt key.

By doing this you are indicating an offset to Photoshop. If you dragged the mouse 70 pixels up and 42 pixels to the left, then it will "paint" using material 70 pixels down and 42 pixels to the right of the brush. You are not restricted to copying to and from the areas indicated when setting the offset. It is possible to paint anywhere on the screen using this offset, but with the proviso that the source must be somewhere on the image. If the position of the brush is such that the source area is taken beyond the edge of the image, there is nothing to clone and nothing is "painted" onto the screen.

Blending in

It is necessary to apply some common sense when using the Clone tool. Look at the image to find a source that will convincingly cover the object or blemish that is to be removed. In general it is best to use source material that is quite close to the area that will be covered. Material from further afield often looks as though it is suitable, but when you try it there are problems. In most images there are variations in the general level of brightness from one area to another. This can result in the cloned material being noticeably lighter or darker than its immediate surroundings. Like everything else in a photograph, textures and patterns tend to get smaller as they recede into the distance. If a pattern is obviously larger or smaller than its surroundings it will look like a patched area of the photograph.

Fig.7.14 The object in its original position

The direction of any pattern is another important consideration. In this example the pattern in the lake runs horizontally throughout. There will often be variations though, and a common example is where a portrait has a blemish in the subject's hair. The lines in the hair will run in various directions, and the blemish must be patched using cloned material that runs at something very close to the correct angle. Again, material close to the blemish is more likely to give convincing results than material copied from further afield.

It is often necessary to copy from more than one source in order to produce convincing results. Even when dealing with background material, copying a large amount from one area to another can produce a fairly obvious duplication. Using more than one source often produces more convincing results anyway. In the case of the unwanted objects in the lake, a mixture of cloning from above, below, and one side produced quite good results. An advantage of the clone tool is that it can produce very quick results, and retouching the pelican photograph took less than a minute.

When using the clone tool it is important to bear in mind that it copies from the image as it is when you start each cloning operation. This point is demonstrated by Figure 7.14 and 7.15. Figure 7.14 shows the unwanted object in its original position, and in Figure 7.15 it has been painted out using material copied just to the right of its original position. However, I have continued painting towards the left, and the object has reappeared to the left of its original position. Even though the object was not visible on the screen when it was cloned, it was still in the computer's memory, and it was still copied to the new position.

Of course, this could be useful if you need

Fig.7.15 The Clone tool has moved the object

to move something slightly, but it also means that in most situations there is a definite limit on the amount of material that can be cloned in a single operation. The smaller the offset used, the smaller the amount that can be copied without cloning the object you are trying to cover. Results are often best with a small offset, but a large offset has the advantage of enabling each operation to clone more material. A compromise therefore has to be sought. If circumstances force the use of a small offset, it is still possible to use a small amount of source material to fill a large area. However, it has to be done in several clone operations rather than one large one.

It is desirable to clone material in as few operations as possible as this makes it quick and easy to produce seamless results. In practice this is not an option if a small offset is used, and copying large areas runs the

Fig.7.16 It is easy to copy from one image to another, but difficult to get convincing results

risk of making the use of cloning too obvious. Due care has to be taken when using numerous small cloning operations to fill a large area. It is easier to end up with odd looking repeating patterns than it is to produce convincing results. Varying the direction and size of the offset helps to avoid or at least disguise any repeating patterns.

Alignment option

When trying to make a small amount of source material go a long way it can be useful to remove the tick in the Alignment checkbox of the Options bar. As already explained, the Clone tool normally operates using the offset indicated by pressing the Alt key and dragging the pointer. This offset is used wherever you "paint" on the screen. It can be changed at any time by pressing the Alt key and dragging the pointer again, but it can be tedious and time consuming if numerous changes are required.

Things operate rather differently with the Alignment option switched off. Before using the Clone tool it is merely necessary to press the Alt key and then left-click on the centre of the area that you wish to copy from. Each time you start painting with the Clone tool it will start copying from the point that you indicated. In effect, a new offset is indicated and used each time you start using the Clone tool. Simply press the Alt key and left-click on a different point in order copy from a different part of the image. Obviously this method can be very useful when it is necessary to copy the same object to various points on the image.

Note that the Clone tool is not restricted to copying from one part of an image to another. With two images loaded into Photoshop it is possible to set a start position for the copying in one image and then copy to another image. In Figure 7.16 one of the pelicans in the pelicans photograph has been copied to the photograph of the castle ruins using this method. Although the transplanted pelican is in the foreground, it is still rather too big. The Copy and Paste method is often better as it permits scaling and other transformations.

Another problem in this example is that the pelican is backlit but the castle ruins are lit from the front, which demonstrates the point that this type of thing is often less than convincing whatever method is used. Things like filling small blemishes using material from another print and copying a cloud to an otherwise cloudless sky are usually successful, but it can be difficult to obtain good results when trying anything more ambitious. It can be done, but you have to be careful with the choice of source material, and the cut and paste method is usually better.

When undertaking any complex cloning it is a good idea to operate the appropriate button in the History palette and take snapshots at various stages in the development of the work. If things start to go awry it is then easy to go back to an earlier stage where things were progressing nicely. It is just a matter of left-clicking on the entry for the appropriate snapshot. Of course, the History palette enables the image to be taken back 20 steps without the use of snapshots, but you can soon find that more than 20 cloning operations have been used.

Other options

With the All Layers checkbox ticked it is possible to copy from any visible layer to the current layer. This checkbox is not ticked by default, and it is then only possible to copy from the current layer. The Mode menu (Figure 7.17) gives a long list of alternatives to straightforward cloning, and this is available with any brush tool selected. Some of these are fairly obvious in the way that they function, while others are something less than obvious

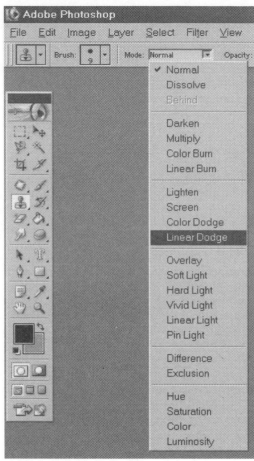

Fig.7.17 The Mode menu offers a variety of blend modes

in this respect. The best way to get to grips with them is to go through the complete list, trying them one by one.

The Luminosity option is quite useful, and it simply applies the luminosity values of the cloned material while retaining the colour values of the original image. The Color option has the opposite effect, with the luminosity values of the original image being retained and only the colour being copied. This can produce some good ghostly effects. In fact a number of the options produce ghostly effects. Try the Soft Light, Lighten, and Darken options for example.

The Opacity control might be better termed the Transparency control, and it gives normal operation at 100 percent and an invisibly copy at zero percent. It is sometimes possible to blend the cloned material into the original more convincingly if less than 100 percent opacity is used. With the Alignment option used, it is possible to set a low opacity value and gradually built up the cloned material to the required strength by repeatedly copying it. One slight problem in using less than 100 percent opacity is that it can result in textures in the cloned area of the image being smoothed out.

*Fig.7.18   A selection of brushstrokes.   The one in the centre-left area is
          a wet edge type*

This is almost certain to occur if the cloned material is brought up to the
required opacity by copying it from more than one source. There tends
to be a sort of averaging process that will certainly alter textures and can
lose them altogether.

Flow control

There is also a Flow control, and this is not quite the same as the Opacity
control. With the opacity set at (say) 10 percent, using the Clone tool
once it is only possible to get 10 percent opacity no matter how many
times the brush is used over an area. The Flow control determines the
flow of "paint" from the brush, and at a setting of 10 percent it will only
give about 10 percent opacity with the brush moved over an area once.
However, repeatedly taking the brush over an area will gradually build
up the cloned image, rather like using a low opacity setting and several
separate cloning operations.

*Fig.7.19 This image has a bad scratch near the bottom right-hand
corner*

Note though, that simply placing the brush over an area and holding down the left mouse button will not result in the image gradually building up. It is the number of times that the brush is swept over an area that determines the strength of the cloned image. However, you can get this effect by operating the Airbrush button and using a low flow setting. This method gives the greatest control over the mixing of the original and cloned material, but it requires a bit more skill to fully utilize its potential. It is especially useful if you are using a pointing device that is not pressure sensitive, and otherwise provides little control over the flow of paint.

There are further variations available from the Brush palette, and it is a good idea to try some of these. In Figure 7.18 the strokes at the top and bottom are respectively the normal and fuzzy edged varieties. The one in the middle was produced using the Wet Edge option, which gives a sort of watercolour brush effect, with the "paint" thick at the edges and semi-transparent towards the middle. The stroke to the right of this was

Fig.7.20 A zoomed view showing the scratch and the patch

produced using a brush having a fuzzy edge with the Noise option selected. For most retouching work the normal and fuzzy edged brushes will suffice, but there is a vast range of alternatives available should you need them.

Patch tool

While it is certainly true that the Clone tool is great for painting out unwanted objects and patching blemishes in prints, after using it for some time you soon become aware of some shortcomings. It can be difficult to get the colour and luminosity accurate, and it can also be awkward to match repeating patterns and textures. These are not really problems with the Clone tool itself, but are more inherent limitations of this way of doing things. Life would be much easier if the Clone tool could automatically match the cloned material to the area around the object or blemish that is being removed.

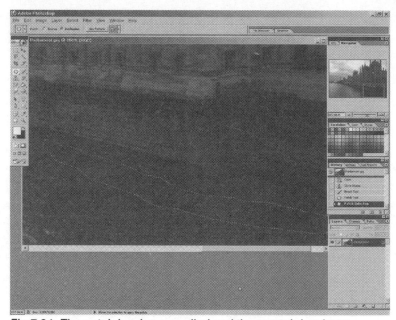

Fig.7.21 The patch has been applied and the scratch has been covered successfully

As yet there is no ideal tool that will invisibly mend any selected part of an image. Perhaps this will appear somewhere around Photoshop 15! However, Photoshop 7 does have a couple of tools that go some way to providing better removal of blemishes and unwanted objects. These are the Healing Brush tool, which is a variation on the Clone tool, and the Patch tool. As one might expect, they are grouped together in the Toolbox, but they are separate from the Clone Stamp tool (which is grouped with the Pattern Stamp tool). We will consider the Patch tool first.

The Patch tool uses material from an area indicated by the user to cover the blemish or object that must be removed. In the contrived example of Figure 7.19 there is a bad scratch on the image near the bottom right-hand corner. In Figure 7.20 the appropriate part of the image has been enlarged using the Zoom tool, and an area just below the scratch has been selected using the Patch tool. By default the Patch tool provides the Lasso tool so that the user can select an area to use as a patch, but you are not restricted to this selection method. It is possible to switch to another selection tool and utilize any of the normal selection techniques. If preferred, the selection can be made prior to entering the Patch tool.

Fig.7.22 A view of the full image with no sign of the scratch

In the Options bar there are two radio buttons marked Source and Destination. In this example we are selecting the source material for the patch first, and the Source button must therefore be selected when doing this. With the source material selected, the Destination button is operated and the patch is dragged to the destination. The patch can only be dragged with the pointer placed within the selected area, and the pointer will change slightly to indicate that dragging is possible. Release the left mouse button to drop the patch in place, and the scratch will be covered over (Figure 7.21). Figure 7.22 shows the screen with the image zoomed out to fill the screen again, and the scratch has vanished.

In this example the source was defined first, and then the source material was applied to the destination. Photoshop permits things to be done the other way around, with the destination being defined first. The selection is then moved to another area, which is used as the source and applied to the destination. In Figure 7.23 the Destination button has been operated and an area around the scratch has been selected. The Source button was then operated, and the selection was dragged a little way down the image. The selection jumped back to its original position

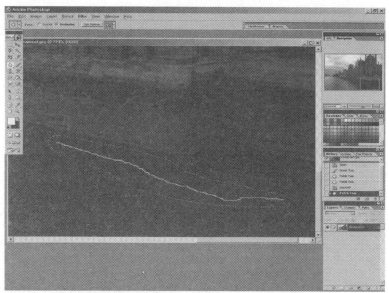

Fig.7.23 The area around the scratch has been selected

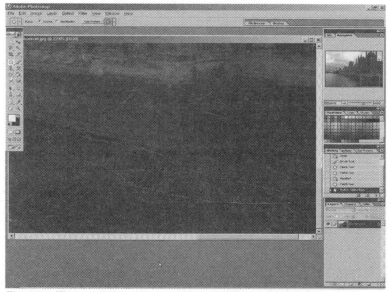

Fig.7.24 The patch has been applied and the scratch is covered

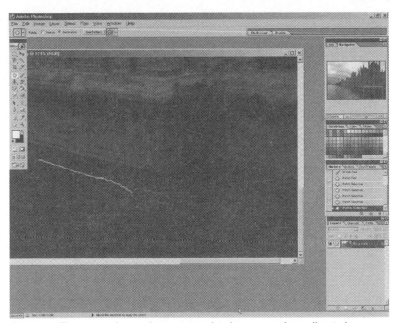

Fig.7.25 The scratch can be removed using several small patches

when the left mouse button was released, but it took the source material with it. As before, the patch has been successfully applied to the blemish (Figure 7.24).

All in one

This second method is easier in cases where a large patch is required and it is to be applied in one go. By drawing around the blemish using the Lasso tool you are certain of producing a patch of suitable shape. Drawing the selection even slightly offset from blemish runs the risk of producing one that is not quite the right shape. It may then fail to cover the blemish correctly when the patch is applied. Note that it is not necessary to patch an area in a single operation. In Figure 7.25 a small source selection has been made and then dragged to various positions on the scratch, gradually nibbling away at it.

Although it works fine with scratches, this method may not be so effective with wider patches. This is due to the way the Patch tool tries to blend the source material with the destination. This is usually an advantage,

Fig.7.26 The cloned material is much darker than its surroundings

but it can be counterproductive. Figures 7.26 and 7.27 show the way in which the Patch tool tries to meld the patch with the destination material. In Figure 7.26 the dinghy to the left of a fishing boat has been selected, together with the areas of the sea that are in the dinghy's shadow or show its reflection. The patch has then been moved to the right-hand side of the fishing boat, but the mouse button has not been released. At this stage that patch is exactly the same as the source material, and it is obviously much darker than destination area.

In Figure 7.27 the mouse button has been released and the source material has been melded into the destination. It is perhaps less than perfect in the sea to the rear of the dinghy, but it is certainly much more convincing with the melding than without it. A few seconds with the Clone was sufficient to seamlessly merge the sea to the rear of the dinghy into its surroundings (Figure 7.28). One slight problem is that the dinghy has been lightened along with the sea, but it is not difficult to correct this type of problem. Two boats would be unlikely to be exactly the same shade anyway, so perhaps this sort of thing will not necessarily be a problem anyway.

Fig.7.27 The cloned material has been melded into its surroundings

Fig.7.28 A small amount of retouching has improved matters

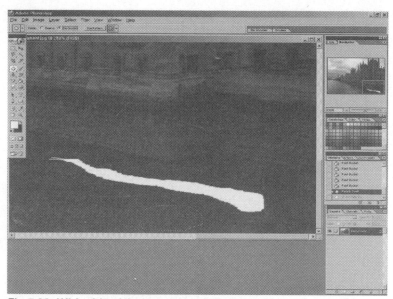

Fig.7.29 Wider blemishes are more difficult to deal with

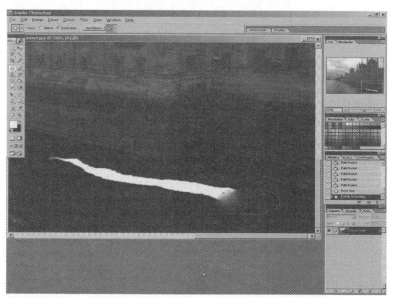

Fig.7.30 The small patch is less than completely successful

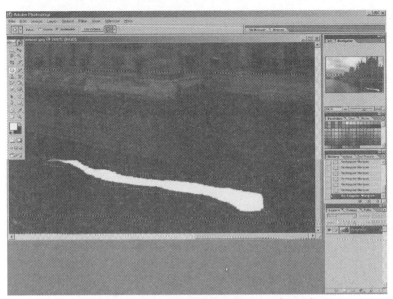

Fig.7.31 The area around the blemish has been selected

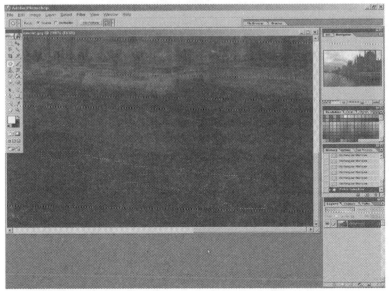

Fig.7.32 Patching the blemish in one operation works much better

Fig.7.33 Once again, the source material is too dark

The melding can be counterproductive when there is anything wider than a scratch and the patch is applied piece by piece. This effect is demonstrated by Figures 7.29 and 7.30. Here the blemish is clearly much wider than a scratch. In Figure 7.29 the source for a small patch has been selected, and in Figure 7.30 it has been applied to one end of the blemish. Unfortunately, Photoshop can not distinguish the normal material from the blemish, so it has melded the blemish into the patch. This does not happen if the blemish is patched in one operation, as in Figure 7.31 and 7.32. The patch is blended into the surrounding area, so the blemish is not taken into account.

The same problem can occur if the patch is applied next to a contrasting area. It will meld convincingly on the sides where there is low contrast, but merge rather obviously on the sides where there is high contrast. Of course, this might be the effect you are after, but in most cases it will make the patch ineffective. It is then better to opt for an alternative method of retouching.

Fig.7.34 Photoshop has melded the cloned material into its surroundings

Healing tool

On trying the Healing tool it will probably seem to work in exactly the same way as the standard Clone Stamp tool. However, it actually combines the melding characteristics of the Patch tool with the copying ability of the Clone tool. This is demonstrated by Figures 7.33 and 7.34. Here the dinghy has again been copied to the right-hand side of the fishing boat, and in Figure 7.33 the left mouse button has not yet been released. The cloned dinghy and surrounding sea are therefore in their original form.

In Figure 7.34 the mouse button has been released and the melding has been applied. As before, the cloned material has been made much lighter so that it merges into the new surroundings much better. In this example the Healing tool was used to clone an object, but it can be used to paint over unwanted objects or imperfections. The same melding technique will be used in an attempt to merge the cloned material more convincingly into the surrounding material. Like the Clone tool, it is used more for removing blemishes than for copying objects.

Pattern

Both the Healing and Patch tools have a Pattern option which is available via a checkbox in the Options bar. With this option selected the normal cloning action is no longer obtained, and these tools instead put preset patterns onto the image. Various patterns are available from the pop-down menu, and further patterns can be loaded via the submenu (Figure 7.35). The basic idea is to have patterns to suit various types of repair that you carry out frequently. These could be various skin tones, patterns taken from landscapes, or whatever.

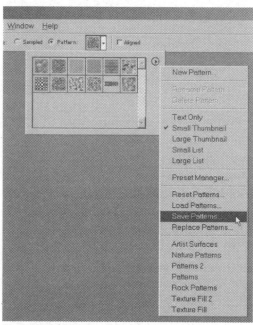

A good range of patterns are included with Photoshop, but looking at things realistically you will need to define your own in order to properly utilise this facility. Defining your own patterns is very simple, and the first step is to select a rectangular area that contains the pattern. Note that the area selected must be a rectangle, so only use the rectangular version of the Marquee tool to make the selection. Next select the Define Pattern option from the Edit menu. A small dialogue box will appear, and a name for the pattern is entered here. Left-click the OK button when you have finished entering the name, and then activate the Pattern menu. The newly created pattern should have been added to the menu.

Fig.7.35 Numerous patterns are available

The Pattern option is useful, but like all the brush tools is has to be used sensibly. It works best with small areas. The problem in covering a

Fig.7.36 The dinghy near the top right-hand corner has been darkened

large area with a pattern is that it has to be used over and over again, which will often produce a tiling effect. This is fine if you require a tiling effect, but in most cases it is definitely not what is required.

In theory it is the pattern and not the colour of the pattern that is important. Photoshop will always try to match the colour of the pattern to match the surrounding area. Photoshop is actually very good at matching the colour, but in practice it might not be totally successful in every case. The chances of obtaining good results are better if the pattern starts off with something vaguely like the correct colour. Of course, black and white in the pattern will remain black and white once the pattern has been melded into an image.

Dodge and Burn

Dodge and burn are two terms used when making photographic prints by hand. Dodging is when card masks or the operator's hands are used to block light from the enlarger to prevent it from reaching certain parts of the photographic paper. This in only done for part of the exposure,

Fig.7.37   The original version of the photograph

and its purpose is to reduce the exposure to parts of the print. Burning is the opposite process, where the print is exposed normally, and then extra exposure is used on certain parts of the print. On the face of it, burning makes areas lighter, and dodging makes them darker. It is actually the other way around though, because the prints are normally made from photographic negatives onto negative printing paper. Therefore, burning makes areas darker and dodging makes them lighter.

In an earlier example a dinghy and the surrounding sea was copied to a lighter part of the image, and Photoshop duly lightened the cloned sea to match the destination. Unfortunately, in doing so it also lightened the dinghy, making it rather too light. The Burn tool is ideal for correcting this sort of thing. It is just a matter of selecting a suitable brush type and size, and then "painting" over the light part of the image until it has been darkened sufficiently. Compare the darkened version of Figure 7.36 with the original version (Figure 7.28).

You will often find that the effect of the Burn tool is too strong, but its effect can be reduced via the Exposure control on the Options bar. To

Fig.7.38 The shadow areas have been lightened using the dodge tool

reduce the effect, use a lower setting than the default value of 50 percent. It might occasionally be better to have the Burn tool provide a stronger effect by increasing the exposure value. The Range menu permits the burning to be applied principally to the shadows, mid tones, or highlights. An increase in contrast can be produced by applying burning to the shadow areas.

The Dodge tool has the same controls as the Burn type and is much the same in use except, of course, it lightens rather than darkens. The main use for the Dodge tool is in lightening excessively dark shadow areas. Strong shadows tend to be a problem whenever the light is provided by a single source, such as the sun on a cloudless day. This can give problems with things like a shadow under the bride's nose making it look like she has a moustache! Modern films have good colour saturation, but this seems to have been achieved at the expense of ever higher levels of contrast. Consequently, digital images produced by scanning prints, negatives, or transparencies often have a definite lack of detail in the shadow areas.

Moderate use of the Dodge tool will sometimes help to bring out a little more detail in the shadows, and will prevent shadow areas from looking excessively "heavy". Figure 7.37 shows part of the photograph of the artist painting the seascape. The photographs in this book have been subjected to a certain amount of contrast reduction in order to accommodate the printing process, so the shadows on the original image are even darker than those in Figure 7.37. In Figure 7.38 some lightening of the shadows has been applied using the Dodge tool. Avoid excessive use of the Dodge tool, as it will provide rather washed out colours. The opposite is true of the Burn tool, which will produce oversaturated colours if you are not careful.

It is not a good idea to immediately opt for the Dodge tool when dealing with excessively dark areas. As demonstrated previously, some processing using the Levels or Curves facilities will usually provide good overall brightness and avoid this type of problem. The Dodge tool is best for localised problems that can not be fixed using these facilities. Also, bear in mind that an area can be selected, and adjustments to brightness, contrast, and colour balance can be applied to that area.

Sponge tool

The Sponge tool is grouped with the Dodge and burn tools, and it is often used in conjunction with them. This is a useful tool in its own right though. In its normal (Desaturate) mode the Sponge tool reduces saturation, or weakens colours in other words. I presume the name of this tool is derived from the small sponges that watercolorists sometimes use to remove paint from the paper, giving weaker colours. Darkening an area using the Burn tool often results in excessively strong colours and the Sponge tool will correct this problem. Of course, it can be used wherever an image has problems with over bright-colours.

The Mode menu gives the option of setting the Sponge tool to the Saturate mode, where it has the opposite effect to normal. In other words, it increases the colour saturation. Lightening areas using the Dodge tool often results in washed-out colours, and the Saturate mode can be used to correct this problem. It can also be used wherever there is a localised problem with weak colours. Overall problems with colour saturation are more easily corrected using the Hue/Saturation feature.

Fig.7.39 Lightening the image has produced grain in the dark areas

History Brush

The History Brush is a facility that should not be overlooked. Often it is easier to apply processing to an entire image and then selectively remove, rather than trying to select most of the image and then apply the processing. Another way of using the History Brush is apply selective processing, and then use this tool to tidy things up by removing some of the processing. The History Brush is often used with filter effects, but it can be used to partially undo most types of processing.

In Figure 7.39 the image has been lightened to bring out the texture in the beach, which is actually comprised of millions of cockleshells. This has worked, and it has quite a good early morning misty feel, but the lightening has brought out unwanted grain in some of the darker areas. In Figure 7.40 these darker areas have been returned to their previous state using the History Brush, but the rest of the image is unchanged.

It is not possible to use the History Brush to selectively remove all processing. For example, it is not possible to change from RGB mode to Grayscale mode and then selectively restore colour to the image. The Grayscale mode does not support colour, so there is no way the History Brush can partially restore the colour. There will often be an alternative

Fig.7.40 The dark areas have been returned to their former state

method that will work, and in this case the obvious way around the problem is to produce the greyscale version of the image using the Hue/ Saturation facility. With the saturation at its minimum value the colour is removed and a greyscale image is produced. It is then possible for the History Brush to selectively reintroduce the colour by returning the saturation to its previous value.

Selective processing

Remember that it is possible to less than fully restore processing by using the History Brush with an Opacity setting of less than 100 percent. Remember also, that it is possible to apply some processing, undo it, and then selectively reapply it using the History Brush. The History Brush will selectively redo whatever processing was just undone. This means that you can effectively "paint" on the image using any of the filters, or just about any other processing. You have to go about it in the right way in order to get this to work.

The History Brush is essentially the same as the Clone tool, but it copies from another state instead of the present one. By default the History

Brush will take things back to the state in the snapshot at the top of the History palette. In other words, it takes the affected parts of the image back to their initial state. The state it copies from can be one listed in the History palette in the normal way, or one that you provide by placing a snapshot in the History palette. If you apply some filtering and then undo it, the History Brush will copy from the initial state, prior to the filtering being added. It therefore has no effect, and the pointer will probably have a diagonal line through the normal brush outline. This indicates that the tool is inoperative.

It is possible to alter the state used as the source by left-clicking in the left column of the History palette for that state. The icon

Fig.7.41 The source state can be changed via the History palette

for the History palette will appear in the left column of the selected state (Figure 7.41), so you can see which state will be used as the source. The entry for processing disappears from the History palette if the processing is reversed using the Undo facility. This makes it impossible to use it as the source for the History Brush.

The solution is to add the processing, take a snapshot, reverse the processing, and then use the snapshot as the source for the History Brush. This has been done in Figure 7.42, where the Glass filter was used on the image, removed, and then reinstated on the bottle using the History Brush. Clearly this is not the only way of adding effects selectively, but "painting" them on to the image is often the best method.

Art History

The Art History Brush performs the same basic function as the History Brush, but with added artistic effects. The idea is to use it to add a painterly quality to photographs, and a huge range of effects are on offer. Using the default settings and a small brush size the effect is

Fig.7.42 The effect has only been reapplied to the bottle

relatively small, as shown by Figure 7.43. Here the left half of the image has been left untouched and the right half has been given the Art History Brush treatment. The image of Figure 7.44 was produced in exactly the same way, but using a very large brush size. This is clearly a lot less subtle, and produces a semi-abstract effect.

There are plenty of settings to tinker with on the Options bar when using the Art History Brush (Figure 7.45). The Style menu provides a choice of several styles of brushstroke. The Area value controls the area covered, but also the number of brushstrokes generated. Using a higher Area value results in more brushstrokes being generated. Of course, the brush size also has a large effect on the area covered, so select a suitable brush first and then find the best area setting. The tolerance setting can be used to limit the brush to areas where there is a substantial difference between the source state and the current one. A high value requires a large difference before any "painting" is possible, and a low value permits the Art History Brush to be used anywhere on the image.

Fig.7.43 The effect of the Art History Brush can be quite small...

Fig.7.44 ...but many settings produce extreme results

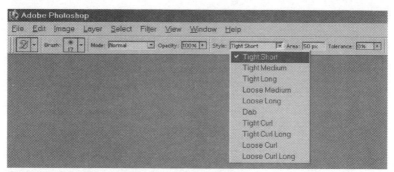

Fig.7.45 A range of stroke styles are available from the Style menu

Fig.7.46 Most stroke styles are lavish

Getting the desired effect using the Art History Brush can be a bit tricky. There are plenty of settings where nothing much happens, and moving even slightly away from these tends to produce quite extreme effects such as the one shown in Figure 7.46. It usually requires some careful adjustments to get the required effect, particularly with relatively low resolution images. The image shown in Figure 7.47 originally had a resolution of just over 1000 pixels for each dimension, but this was increased to just over 2000 pixels before the Art History Brush was

*Fig.7.47 Here the number of pixels was boosted, the processing was
added, and then the number of pixels was returned to
normal. This has helped to tame the Art History Brush*

used. It was then brought back down to 1000 pixels or so after the processing had been added. This made it much easier to produce a relatively restrained effect.

In order to really get to grips with the Art History Brush it is necessary to put in some time experimenting with the various options. Note that many similar effects can be produced using filters, and it is also worth experimenting with the various options available from the Filter menu.

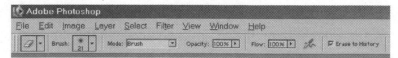

Fig.7.48 The Options bar has an Erase to History option

History eraser

When the Eraser tool is selected there is an Erase to History checkbox in the Options bar (Figure 7.48). When this is ticked, the Eraser tool erases the image and replaces it with the equivalent area of the selected snapshot or state. In other words, it operates much like the History Brush tool. In Figure 7.49 the Art History Brush tool was used with an outsize brush to produce an image that is blurred to the point that there is nothing recognisable. The Eraser tool was then used to restore some of the original image, giving an effect like the flowers being viewed through a steamed-up window with some of the condensation wiped away.

Pressure sensitive

If you are using a graphics tablet with Photoshop it is very likely that it will be pressure sensitive. This facility can be used to good effect with Photoshop's brush tools, and the pressure sensitivity can be used in a variety of ways. Figure 7.50 shows some brush strokes produced using a pressure sensitive stylus, and with some it controls the width of the stroke while with others it controls the flow of "paint". As one of the strokes demonstrates, it is still possible to produces straightforward strokes at maximum width (or whatever), and you are not forced into producing fancy brushstrokes when using a pressure sensitive device.

The facilities available from graphics tablets vary from one unit to another. Units designed primarily for use with CAD systems are often large but may lack pressure sensitivity. For use with Photoshop these are better than a mouse, but a smaller unit that does have pressure sensitivity is much better. Some graphics tablets go beyond pressure sensitivity and permit the angle of the pen to control certain aspects of brushstrokes. The documentation supplied with the tablet should provide details of the facilities available, and how to use them with popular graphics programs, including Photoshop.

With the tablet correctly installed, additional options will be available when using the appropriate tools. Pressure information can be used with some tools that do not really fall into the brush category. Figure 7.51 shows

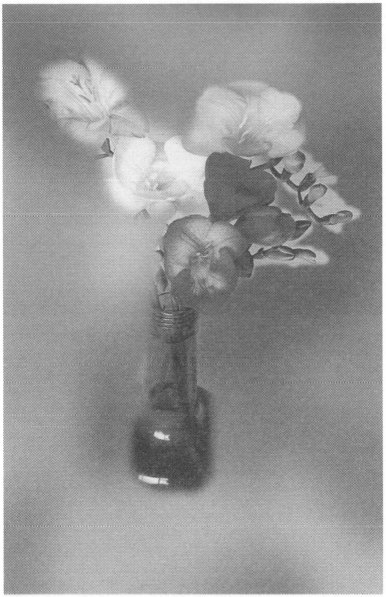

Fig.7.49 The processing has been selectively erased

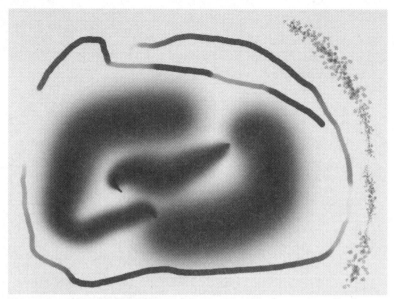

Fig.7.50 Some brushstrokes made using a pressure sensitive stylus

the options bar with the Magnetic Lasso tool selected, and there is a Pen Pressure checkbox. The Edge Width value decreases with increasing pressure when this option is ticked.

Fig.7.51 Where appropriate, a pressure option is provided

Fade Brush Tool

The Fade Brush Tool reduces the opacity of the brush stroke just applied to the image. This is not a history tool, so it is not possible to select a brushstroke in the History palette and then adjust its opacity using this facility. Using another tool, even a non-brush tool such as the Lasso tool, also removes the ability to use this facility on the last brushstroke.

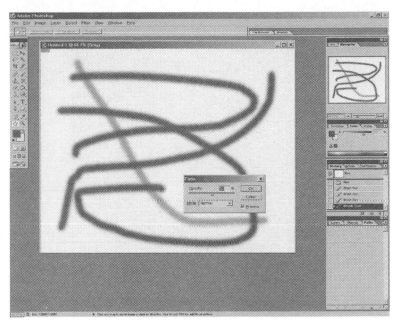

Fig.7.52 The last brushstroke has been faded by 50 percent

Despite its limitations, this facility can be quite useful. It is very easy to use, and it is just a matter of selecting Fade Brush Tool from the Edit menu and adjusting the slider control in the small window that appears.

In Figure 7.52 the brushstrokes were all applied using the same dark grey colour, but the last one added has been faded by about 50 percent. It is also possible to fade strokes produced using the other brush tools. In Figure 7.53 one of the fishing boats and a dinghy have been cloned using the Clone tool, and then they have been faded using the Fade Brush Tool facility. I suppose that this has potential for merging patched areas into the surrounding material more successfully, but there are other methods available in Photoshop that might be better.

Custom brushes

Photoshop has a wide range of brushes as supplied, but it is possible to produce your own custom shapes. One way of doing this is to use all or part of an image, and for this example our earlier heart shape filled with a rose will be used. The outline is selected first, and then the Define

Fig.7.53 Cloned items can be faded like any other brushstrokes

Brush option is selected from the Edit menu. This produces a small dialogue box (Figure 7.54) where a name for the new brush is entered. Operating the OK button creates the brush and adds it to the Brushes palette (Figure 7.55). The entire image is used for the brush if no selection is made prior to defining the new brush.

Figure 7.56 shows some brushstrokes using the new brush. Note that the colours of the source image are not used when you paint with a custom brush. Like the other brushes, it paints using the current foreground colour. It does use the luminosity values and shapes from the source image. This is demonstrated by the short strokes in Figure 7.56, where the mouse has been left-clicked rather than dragged. Each click has produced a clone of the original image but in the current foreground colour. Using this method of producing a custom brush often gives a large brush diameter, and in this example the brush was about 380 pixels in diameter. However, the diameter can be varied in the normal way using the slider control in the Brushes palette.

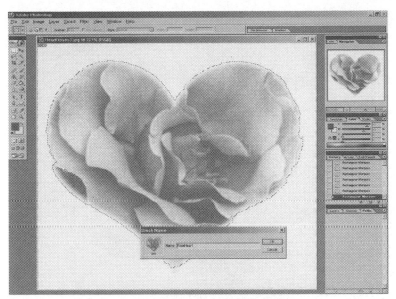

Fig.7.54 A name for the brush is entered in the textbox

In order to make a new brush from scratch, start with a new canvas and then draw the shape using the Brush or Pencil tool and add any required fill. The brush design in Figure 7.57 was produced using the Pencil tool with a fill provided by the Gradient tool. Once the design has been completed, the Define Brush option is selected from the Edit menu, a name for the brush is added in the

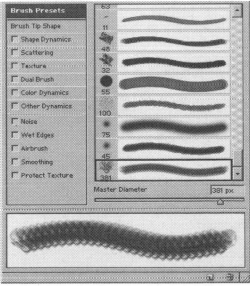

Fig.7.55 The new brush has been added

Fig.7.56 Some brushstrokes produced using the new brush

Fig.7.57 A new brush design produced from scratch

Fig.7.58 Brushstrokes produced using the newly created brush design of Fig.7.57

popup dialogue box, and then the OK button is pressed to complete the operation. It is not necessary to select the outline of the brush prior to defining it. Photoshop will automatically discard any unused canvas around the design. Figure 7.58 shows some strokes produced using the newly defined brush.

With a large range of tools and effects on offer, the brush tools can be a bit bewildering. On the other hand, the basic functions are quite simple, so you can start with some simple tasks and gradually move up to more complicated processing. As with most aspects of Photoshop, experience is important, so be prepared to put in some time and effort experimenting with these tools.

Points to remember

Photographs can be retouched using the ordinary Brush and Pencil tools, but it can be quite difficult to get really convincing results using this method, particularly with anything more than a small area. Copying from another part of the image, or from another image, usually gives better results with far less effort. The Clone, Healing, and Patch tools are used for this type of retouching.

The Clone tool makes a verbatim copy of the source material, although the cloned material can be altered by reducing the Opacity setting and (or) using one of the fancy blend modes. The Healing tool tries to match the cloned material with its surroundings. This usually gives top quality results very quickly, and in many circumstances the Healing tool is better that the Clone type.

With the Patch tool you define an area that is to be used as the patch and then drag it to the area to be patched. Alternatively, the area to be patched is defined, and then it is dragged to the area that will be used to provide the patch. Whichever method is used, Photoshop with try to blend the patch into its surroundings.

The Healing and Patch tools both have a pattern option. Material from a predefined rectangular area is used as the source when this option is used. Photoshop is supplied complete with some patterns, but it is necessary to define your own patterns in order to fully utilize this facility.

The Dodge and Burn tools can be used to respectively make areas lighter and darker. The Sponge tool can be used to increase or decrease the colour saturation of the processed areas. It often has to be used after the Dodge and Burn tools in order to prevent washed-out or over-strength colours.

It is possible to "paint" from a snapshot or earlier state to the current image using the History Brush. This effectively enables filtering and other processing to be selectively added or removed. The action of the Art History Brush is essentially the same, but with added painterly effects.

These effects can easily go completely "over the top", and careful adjustment is usually needed in order to get the desired effect.

A History option is available when using the Eraser tool. This enables parts of the current image to be erased and replaced with an earlier state or snapshot. This makes it easy to selectively remove filtering or other processing.

Photoshop will make use of pressure values produced by a compatible graphics tablet and stylus. The pressure value can be used to control such things as the width of strokes, the flow value of brushes, and the Width setting of the Magnetic Lasso tool.

A large range of predefined brushes are available in Photoshop, but you can easily define your own , All or part of an existing image can be used as the basis of a brush or you can design one from scratch. Custom brushes "paint" in the normal way using the current foreground colour rather than any colours used in the brush design.

7 Brush tools

Filters and text

Artistic filtering

Photoshop has a huge range of built-in filters, and there are plenty more available if you need even more. Most of these filters are what would be termed effects filters in normal photographic terms. This makes them of relatively little value for those simply wishing to use Photoshop to get the best possible technical quality from their photographs. On the other hand, if you are into that type of thing and would like to be more creative with your images, the Filter menu will probably be your favourite part of Photoshop.

Fig.8.1 The non-filtered version of the photograph

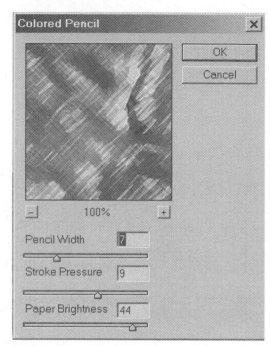

Fig.8.2 The control panel for the Colour Pencil filter

Even those having little interest in filter effects would be well advised to spend a little time experimenting with a selection of filters. It is quite good fun and you might just find an effect that will be useful. Many of the filters are designed to effectively turn a photograph into a painting or drawing. Figure 8.1 shows a photograph of the furry friend who likes to sleep on my computer monitor during the winter months. Strong textures like those in his fur are often good candidates for drawing of painting effects. For this example I selected the Colored Pencil filter, which is in the Artistic submenu of the Filter menu. This produced the control panel of Figure 8.2, where there are three sliders that can be used to vary the effect. This is typical of the Photoshop filters, but different filters require different controls.

The names of the controls give good clues to their functions, but in the end it is down to the "suck it and see" method. In this case there is a Paper Brightness control. The paper shows through in areas of high luminosity, so the image looks more or less normal using a high value. Setting this slider near zero gives black paper, and therefore black highlights! The Pencil Width setting determines the width of the lines used, with higher values giving broader lines. This effectively acts as a definition control, since wider lines reduce definition. Most of the artistic filters have a control that is broadly similar in its effect. The third control is for Stroke Pressure, and this gives weak colours at low settings and strong colours at high settings.

Fig.8.3 The filtered version of the photograph

Figure 8.3 shows the filtered version of Figure 8.1. If I did not know that it had been produced from a colour photograph I think that I might be fooled into thinking that it was a genuine drawing. In the greyscale reproduction used here it does a reasonable imitation of a drawing done with a graphite stick or something similar. Note that the image does not respond to changes in the controls until the OK button is operated and the filtering is applied. Even using a fast computer it usually takes several seconds for the effect to be applied to the image.

However, there is a small preview section in the control panel that

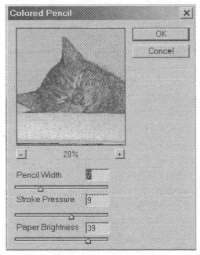

Fig.8.4 The zoom level of the control panel is adjustable

shows part of the image, and this does respond to the controls in real-time, or as close as Photoshop and your computer can get to real-time operation. At a scale of 100 percent it is only possible for the preview panel to show a small part of the image. It can be useful to use a lower scale in order to show more of the image (Figure 8.4). The preview resolution is relatively low, but it gives a good overall impression of what the filtered image will look like. Use the small + button below the preview image to increase the scale, or the – button to reduce it. It is possible to pan

Fig.8.5 Artistic filtering works well with a painterly image

around the image by placing the pointer over the preview panel. The pointer then changes to the pan (hand) icon, and the image can be dragged in the normal way.

Some of the simpler filters do actually permit the effect to be applied to the image in real-time. The preview panel is still available, but where possible it is much better to tick the Preview checkbox and view the changes on the image itself. A few of the more complex filters lack any form of preview facility. It is then a matter of using trial and error, with the aid of the Undo facility, until the desired effect is obtained.

There are other arty effects available in the Artistic, Sketch, and Brush Strokes submenus, and it is worth experimenting with all of these. Some of the best results are produced from photographs that already have

Fig.8.6 The filtered version of the image. The Paint Daubs filtering has produced quite a good effect which is even better in the original colour version

Fig.8.7 Solarizing looks quite dramatic even in a greyscale version

some painterly qualities. The picture of Tower Bridge at night shown in Figure 8.5 certainly falls into that category, particularly the reflections in the river and the lighter parts elsewhere. Using the Paint Daubs filter usually provides good results with this type of image, and Figure 8.6 shows the image with this filter used quite strongly. It looks much more spectacular in colour, but even in greyscale reproduction the effect is quite good.

Other filter effects available include distortion filters that produce such things as "fisheye" lens effects, glass distortions, and so on. The Stylise menu has some of the more extreme filters, including the popular Solarize and Glowing Edges. These are shown in Figures 8.7 and 8.8 respectively. They actually work quite well in greyscale, but the Glowing Edges effect is much more potent with colour reproduction.

Fig.8.8 The Glowing Edges filter produces an interesting effect

Extract

Not all the filters are what could really be termed effects or special effects types, and the Extract filter is certainly not in the effects category. It provides filtering in the normal sense of filtering out the bits that you do not need. It is more like a selection tool than a Photoshop filter, but the filtered material is not a selection and can not be skewed, scaled, etc. At least, it can not be used with these transformations until it has been turned into a true selection, which is clearly an easy task once everything else on that layer has been filtered out. The Extract filter is available direct from the Filter menu, and the new window of Figure 8.9 is launched when this option is selected.

The first task is to paint around the edge of the object or objects that you wish to retain. The stroke must cover the edge of each object and the

Fig.8.9 The Extract filter uses this large window

background. In this example the three roses are to be retained and everything else is to be removed. The Edge Highlighting tool is used to add the outlines, and it is the default tool when using the Extract filter. Its button is the top one in the Extract window's version of the Toolbox, which is in the top left-hand corner of the window. The Eraser tool is available beneath this, so it is easy to tidy up any mistakes that are made. Figure 8.10 shows the roses duly outlined. The lines do not show up well in the greyscale reproduction of Figure 8.10, but they are in a sort of Day-Glo green that shows up clearly on most images. Red and blue options are available from the Highlight menu in the right-hand section of the window. There is a Smart Highlighting option available via a checkbox, and this operates in a manner that is similar to the Magnetic Lasso tool.

Once the highlighting has been completed it is time to fill the outlines using the Paint Bucket tool, which operates much like the normal version of this tool. Note that the tools in the Extract window must be used, and that the normal Photoshop tools are inoperative until this window closes. Adding a fill might seem to be pointless, but in outlining the areas to be

Fig.8.10 The three roses have been outlined

retained it is possible that other areas will be inadvertently outlined. This is quite likely to occur where there are several areas close together that must be retained. Photoshop will ignore any islands that are not filled.

There is a Preview button that can be used to check the result of the filtering, and it is a good idea to use this option rather than just applying the filtering. Using the Toolbox it is possible to zoom and pan around the image (Figure 8.11) to check that the edges have been detected with adequate accuracy. Material can be trimmed back using the Cleanup tool, or reinstated by using the Cleanup tool while holding down the Alt key. The Edge Touchup can be used to give a sharper and better defined edge. Its basic action seems to be adding opacity to the edge of objects. A smaller brush size will usually be needed when making fine adjustments to the outlines, and the brush size can be adjusted by entering a value into the appropriate text box or using the popup slider control. The zoom, pan, and brush size adjustment controls are all available in the normal mode of the Extract window, and they can be useful if small objects have to be outlined. Operate the OK button once the objects have been

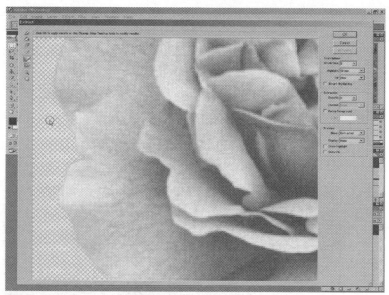

Fig.8.11 It is possible to use pan and zoom controls

Fig.8.12 The three roses have been extracted successfully

extracted with sufficient accuracy, and Photoshop will then return to the normal window (Figure 8.12).

Blurring

Photoshop has a range of blur filters, and it is also possible to produce blurring using other tools such as the Art History Brush. There are also Blur and Smudge tools, with the latter providing a much stronger blurring effect. On the face of it, tools and filters to make your images less sharp are the last thing that you need. However, blurring all or part of an image can be beneficial.

Fig.8.13 The original version of the squirrel photograph

Photographers have for many years used soft focus filters that provide a mixture of a sharp image and a seriously out of focus image. This type of thing is particularly popular for portraits, where the overall effect is quite pleasing and wrinkles and other skin blemishes miraculously disappear.

Sports photographers often use powerful telephoto lenses that have wide apertures, and this combination gives an extremely narrow depth of field. Also, the out of focus areas tend to be well and truly out of focus. These factors are normally deemed an advantage rather than a drawback. Sports photographers could have frequent problems with objects in the background seeming to be growing from the heads of the sports persons. With the backgrounds completely out of focus this does not occur. The backgrounds are often so out of focus that they are purely abstract and it is not possible to make out individual objects. This lack of distraction helps to focus attention on the main subject.

Fig.8.14 The background has been blurred

The squirrel photograph of Figure 8.13 was taken using a powerful telephoto lens, but with the lens well stopped down. The background is well out of focus, but it is still a bit distracting. It is more distracting in the original colour version than in the greyscale conversion, due to the bright greens on the tree trunks. These stand out from the rest of the image, which is otherwise composed almost entirely of browns and greys. Blurring the background while leaving the squirrel and the tree intact is not difficult using Photoshop. There are several approaches that can be used, and in this example the image was first copied to a second layer. This can be achieved by selecting Duplicate Layer from the Layer menu, or dragging the Background layer to the New Layer button on the Layers palette.

The next task is to blur the background on the Background layer. There are several ways of doing this, but the obvious one of selecting Blur from the Blur submenu is unlikely to have much effect. The Blur option is designed to give a slight blurring of material that is quite sharp. Its effect on the parts of images that are already blurred is quite small. The Blur More option provides a stronger effect, but it is still inadequate for this task.

The Gaussian Blur option provides a variable degree of blurring and would certainly do the job, but when used strongly it tends to produce featureless results. In some cases an almost plain background is just what is needed, but was not really what I was looking for in this case. The Smudge tool provided better results, but in the end I settled for an effect obtained using the Art History Brush (Figure 8.14). This has produced the desired effect in the background, but it has also obliterated some of the tree trunk and a fair proportion of the squirrel. These were reinstated by removing the background on the other layer using the Extract facility. Placing the second layer over the Background layer produces the result shown in Figure 8.15.

Fig.8.15 The tree and squirrel have been reinstated

The new background has nothing recognisable to act as a distraction, but it is not so plain as to look totally unnatural.

Gaussian Blur

The Gaussian Blur option mentioned previously is useful for adding anything from a slight blurring to a very strong effect like viewing things through ground glass. It is excellent for blurring backgrounds, and in this example it is the background of the photograph shown in Figure 8.16 that will be blurred. The photograph is reasonable as it stands, but the strong contrasts and textures in the cockleshells slightly overpower the main subject, which is a turnstone incidentally. This is more noticeable on the original colour print where the high contrasts in the shells also tend to make the bird appear to have slightly "soft" focussing. It is actually quite sharp, and it is the subject matter that gives the slightly "soft" look.

Fig.8.16 The original version of the turnstone photograph

Strictly speaking it is not the foreground that has to be processed, since the shells are in the foreground, middle ground, and background. It is everything except the turnstone that has to be given the blurring treatment. I started by selecting the outline of the turnstone using the Magnetic Lasso tool, and then refined it slightly in the Quick Mask mode. The Inverse option in the Select menu was then used to select everything outside the outline. It was then just a matter of applying the required amount of Gaussian Blur filtering. This filter permits the effect to be previewed on the image, and very strong blurring can be applied if desired (Figure 8.17). In this case it is something a bit more subtle that is required, and Figure 8.18 shows the finished image. Particularly in the original colour image, the bird stands out from the background much better.

Bear in mind that blurring is not the only way of dealing with overbearing backgrounds. A reduction in contrast is a useful alternative, and this method has been used with the image shown in Figure 8.19. The contrast in the turnstone has been increased using the Auto Contrast facility. This has worked quite well with the greyscale version of the image, and in my opinion at any rate; it works better than the blurred version. With the colour images though, it is definitely the blurred version that gives the

Fig.8.17 It is possible to completely blur the background

Fig.8.18 A small amount of blurring gives the desired effect

Fig.8.19 Here the background's contrast has been reduced slightly

best result. If a plain background is needed, it can be produced by reducing the contrast to zero. This has been done in Figure 8.20 by using the same setting for the lower set of slider controls in the Levels window. Move the sliders to the left for a darker grey, or to the right for a lighter grey. Alternatively, with the textures removed from the background it is easy to add any desired colour using the Paint Bucket tool.

Soft focus

The Gaussian Blur filter is useful for adding a soft focus effect. It is important to realise that a soft focus effect is not the same as simply blurring the image slightly. Simply adding some Gaussian Blur filtering produces a blurred image and not a soft focus effect. A soft focus effect is produced by having a mixture of a sharp image and one that is very blurred. Photographers often improvise soft focus filters by smearing Vaseline onto a plain glass filter, with the degree of softness being varied by using more or less Vaseline, as required. A popular method in the early days of photography was to use a diffraction grating, which usually meant taping material from a pair of stockings over the lens!

Fig.8.20 Using zero contrast gives a plain background

Both of these methods give the required combination of a blurred image and a sharp one, but lack precise control. Using Photoshop it is easy to use any degree of soft focussing. By keeping a copy of the sharp image it is possible to change your mind and use a less soft effect, which is something that can not be done if the filtering is used when the picture is taken. For this example the soft focussing effect will be added to the rose photograph, and the first step is to apply the Gaussian Blur filtering. This is obtained via the Blur submenu of the Filter menu.

Using too little blur filtering is a common error when adding a soft focus effect. If any detail is still visible in the blurred image, mixing it with the sharp image produces a blurred image rather than a soft focus effect. It is preferable to have the broad areas of colour retained from the original image, but all detail must be lost in the blurring. Do not take the filtering so far that a virtually plain image is produced. Adding a totally blurred image with a sharp one tends to produce a loss of contrast with a relatively weak soft focus effect. Something like the degree of filtering shown in Figure 8.21 should give good results.

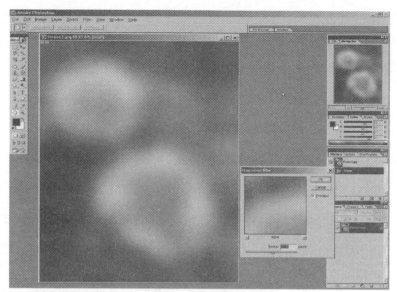

Fig.8.21 A large amount of blurring must be used

Fig.8.22 A mild soft focus effect has been used here

Fig.8.23 A stronger soft focus effect can also be obtained

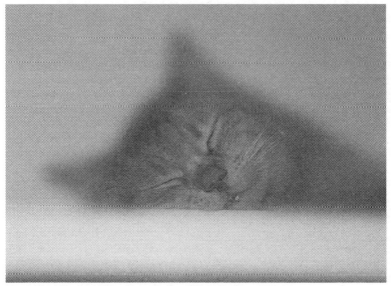

Fig.8.24 The blur filtering can be selectively removed

Fig.8.25 There are two slider controls for Smart Blur filtering

With the blurring added, it is very easy to mix it with the sharp image. Select Fade Gaussian Blur from the Edit menu and then adjust the slider control in the popup control panel to obtain desired effect. Greater fading provides a weaker effect. Fig.8.22 shows the rose image with a weak effect, while in Figure 8.23 the fading has been greatly reduced and a very "soft" image has been obtained. A more versatile effect can be used by using the History Brush to selectively reduce the blurring, as in the example of Figure 8.24. Use the Airbrush option and a very low Flow setting of about 5 percent so that there is good control over the removal of the filtering.

Smart Blur

The Smart Blur filter is a very useful one that often provides a good alternative to soft focus effects. Its basic effect is to blur the image apart from the edges it detects. This form of filtering is mush used by portraitists because of its ability to remove fine marks and patterns, and thus "take years off" the sitter. It can be used in most situations where a smoother

Fig.8.26   The textures have gone in the filtered version of the image

and softer appearance is required. There are two slider controls for this
filter (Figure 8.25), and a preview panel, but no option to preview the
effect on the image itself.

The Threshold control determines the degree of contrast required for
Photoshop to deem something an edge. Few outlines are produced
using a high setting, while practically everything is taken as an outline at
low settings. The Mode menu has two options that permit the outlines to
be viewed on the preview panel. In one mode only the outlines are
shown, and in the other mode the outlines are overlaid on the normal
image. It is obviously important that all the main outlines are detected,
but there can also be some unwanted effects if too many are detected.
In most cases it is best to select one of the outline preview modes and
adjust the threshold control so that only the main outlines are detected.

The Radius control effectively governs the amount of blurring that is
added, and it is just a matter of adjusting it for what is felt to be the best
effect. Some of the filters, including the Smart Blur type, have three
quality settings (Low, Medium, and High). With low resolution images it

Fig.8.27 Motion Blur filtering has produce the first 100mph tortoise

will probably not make too much difference which one is used, and with higher resolution images there might still be little difference between the Medium and High settings. However, the time taken to calculate the changes to the image does vary considerably from one setting to the next. Even with a fast computer it can take quite a long time to make the calculations when the High setting is used.

Figure 8.26 shows the Smart Blur filtering added to the rose. The main edges have been identified correctly and quite a good effect has been produced. Objects tend to look as though they are made from china or porcelain when this filtering is used in large amounts, so use it in moderation unless this is the effect you require. Paradoxically, slightly "soft" images often look sharper when this form of blur filtering is applied. This happens because the edges are retained but the slightly blurred details become blurred so much that they disappear. Photoshop provides better ways to deal with "soft" images though.

Fig.8.28 There is plenty of detail but the focussing is a bit "soft"

Sharp filtering

I would guess that anyone who has put a film through a camera has taken a photograph that is something less than completely sharp. The most obvious reason for a lack of sharpness is that the camera was not focussed correctly, but there are other causes. Some cameras are better than others, and some lenses are certainly much better than others. With some cheap cameras it does not make much difference whether the camera is focussed well or badly. The results are poor either way.

What is termed "camera shake" is certainly a major cause of blurred photographs. Many people jerk the camera as they take each photograph, which can significantly reduce the sharpness even when using a fast shutter speed. Fast moving subjects taken using an inadequate shutter speed is another common cause of blurred images. Sometimes the blurring can be largely avoided by panning with the movement. This will usually blur the background, but this helps to give an impression of speed. The Photoshop Motion Blur filter can be applied to a background to give the same effect. In Figure 8.27 the tortoise has

Fig.8.29 The Sharpen filter provides a modest amount of sharpening

been stretched slightly to make it more streamlined, a small amount of Motion Blur filtering has also been added to the tortoise, and a large amount has been added to the background. The result is the world's first tortoise capable of going from 0 to 60mph in less than five seconds!

Another common problem is inadequate depth of field. Wide apertures enable fast shutter speeds to be used, but will usually result in relatively little being genuinely in focus, particularly with telephoto lenses. With a portrait you focus on the subject's eyes and they are properly in focus on the photograph, but the nose and ears are not. As already explained, limited depth of field can have its advantages, but only in the right circumstances. In many instances it is preferable to have as much depth of field as possible.

Blurring an image is easy enough, but sharpening is a different matter. Filtering can certainly make slightly "soft" images look much more acceptable, and it can also increase the apparent depth of field in photographs that are a bit lacking in this respect. If a photograph is well and truly blurred it would be naïve to expect filtering to turn it into a perfect photograph. Even the systems using supercomputers to process images from space can not do that. Sharpness filtering also tends to be

Fig.8.30 The Sharpen Edges filter has also been used here

ineffective with serious camera shake of the type that produces a double-image effect. Using sharpness filtering on images of this type simply gives you two sharper images!

Options

There are four types of sharpening available from the Sharpen submenu, and the first of these is the straightforward Sharpen option. This operates by looking for variations in colour and tone, and it increases the contrast between adjacent pixels where suitable variations are found. All simple methods of image sharpening use essentially the same method, and are really just providing localised increases in contrast. This can give the illusion of greater sharpness, and I suppose that in a way the image is genuinely sharper, but missing detail can not be put back in by sharpness filtering.

The photograph shown in Figure 8.28 is a good example of the type of image that can benefit from sharpening. It is similar to the cat photograph used in some earlier examples, but it was taken using available light rather than with the aid of a flashgun. In the relatively low light levels indoors this has resulted in the camera using a long shutter speed with

Fig.8.31 The Sharpen more filter gives a much stronger effect

the lens wide open. The definition is not that bad and there is a hint of detail in the fur. However, depth of field is lacking and no part of the image is "biting" sharp.

Figure 8.29 shows the effect of using the Sharpen filter. The change is something less than dramatic, but as viewed on the screen of my monitor anyway, there is a definite improvement in the apparent sharpness of the image, particularly in the fur on the top of Jake's head. The effect of the Sharpen filter is relatively mild, but stronger or additional filtering can be used. The Sharpen Edges filter, as its name implies, is primarily intended for giving more clearly defined edges, such as the edges of the computer monitor in the example photograph. This it does very well, but when used in conjunction with the Sharpen filter it will often give a useful improvement in the general sharpness without taking things "over the top".

Figure 8.30 shows the photograph with the Sharpen and Sharpen Edges filtering applied. There is only a subtle difference between this and the version that only has the Sharpen filtering applied, but the combined effect filtering is quite impressive with the image viewed on a monitor in the Actual Pixels mode. Unlike the original image, it looks acceptably sharp and it still looks quite natural. Large amounts of sharpening can

Fig.8.32 The Unsharp Mask filter gives a versatile effect

be applied by using the Sharpen filter two or three times, or by using the Sharpen More filter. Figure 8.31 shows the image with the original sharpening removed and the Sharpen more filter applied.

At the size the image is reproduced here it might look quite impressive, but with a larger print or looking at the photograph on a monitor it is less impressive. It has a slightly artificial look, and patterns of light pixels are starting to appear in places. Any more filtering would certainly produce some rather odd looking results. Unfortunately, sharpening is needed most when an image is reproduced relatively large, but it is when a sharpened image is viewed large that the filtering becomes more obvious. Always use the minimum amount of filtering that provides acceptable sharpness.

Unsharp Mask

The three types of sharpness filtering described so far are handy for those needing a quick and easy solution to a blurred image, but they provide no real control over the filtering. The same is not true of the

Fig.8.33 A high Radius setting can give odd effects

Unsharp Mask filter, which has the customary three controls and preview option (Figure 8.32). The top control is used to set the required amount of filtering, and it covers a range of 1 to 500 percent. A Radius value is set using the middle control, and this controls the number of surrounding pixels that are altered by the sharpening. It is normally necessary to use a low value here in order to obtain an acceptable effect. A low value is particularly important with an image such as the one used here, which has masses of fine detail. A high value tends to give a glowing effect around the edges of objects (Figure 8.33), and it can also produce oversaturated colours. Set the value too low and no significant sharpening is obtained.

The third slider control sets the Threshold, which is the difference needed between pixels before the sharpening with be applied. High values result in Photoshop finding few areas to sharpen. With a low value the filtering is applied almost everywhere on the image, which usually results in patterns of dots starting to emerge from previously plain areas of the image. It can take a fair amount of juggling with the three controls in order to obtain the best results, but it should be possible to obtain a reasonably sharp looking picture provided the original image contains a reasonable amount of detail.

Many professional users head straight for the Unsharp Mask filter when editing any image. No matter how sharp an image is to start with, it is always possible to make it look "crisper" using this facility. Whether it is desirable to do so is another matter. For low definition images that will be used on the Internet there is perhaps a good case to be made for emphasising the fine details which might otherwise be lost. I habitually use sharpening on web images, but not images that will be printed. There is no harm in trying the Unsharp Mask on every image, but there is no point in applying the filtering unless you genuinely like the effect.

Text

It is often desirable to add text to an image, but this was not really a strong point of Photoshop until quite recently. Fortunately, it now offers an excellent range of text facilities. There are vertical and horizontal versions of the Type tool and the same versions of the Type Mask tool are available. The normal type tools produce text in the current

Fig.8.34 A text mask filled with patterns

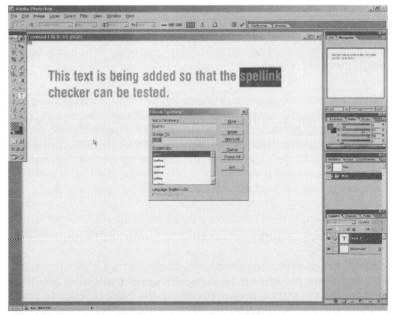

Fig.8.35 Photoshop 7 even has a built-in spelling checker

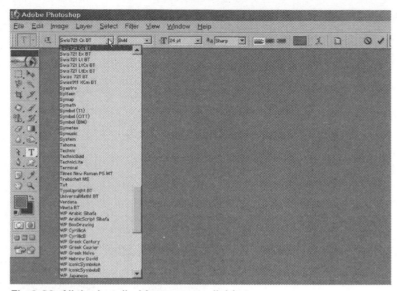

Fig.8.36 All the installed fonts are available

foreground colour, but this can be overridden by selecting a different colour from the Options bar. The mask versions of the Type tool produce masks that can be used in the usual ways, and in Figure 8.34 the mask has been filled with patterns using the Pattern Stamp tool.

Photoshop places each piece of text on its own layer, but text masks are simply placed on the current layer. While normal text remains on its own layer it is readily edited, but there are some restrictions on the way it can be treated. In particular, filters have no effect on text unless it is "rasterized" or rendered, which are the Photoshop terms for converting it into a normal image comprised of pixels. If a text layer is merged with the image it will be rasterized in the process. Once converted to pixels it is possible to apply filters or any of the other processes that can be used with images, but normal text editing is not possible. Make sure the text is correct before you rasterize it, or use any function that will result in it being rasterized.

There is a built-in spelling checker that helps to avoid embarrassing mistakes. It is invoked by selecting the appropriate layer and then choosing Spelling Checker from the Edit menu. This produces a small dialogue box (Figure 8.35), which will show the first error, if it finds any.

Fig.8.37 The text at the top has Strong anti-aliasing

The word in question is also highlighted in the main window. The Photoshop spelling checker uses the normal method of comparing the words in your document with those in its built-in dictionary. The suspect words that are pointed out to the user are those that can not be matched to the dictionary.

Of course, there are plenty of names and other words that for one reason or another are not included in Photoshop's dictionary. You therefore have the option of ignoring the error. In most cases there is also the option of changing it to the suggested alternative, or one of the other alternatives listed. Simply operate the Change button to use the suggested alternative. To use one of the other suggestions, select its entry in the list and then operate the Change button.

Text options

There are a number of choices available from the Options bar when one of the Type tools is selected. These are mostly the sort of thing that you find in word processors or any programs that handle text. The "T" button

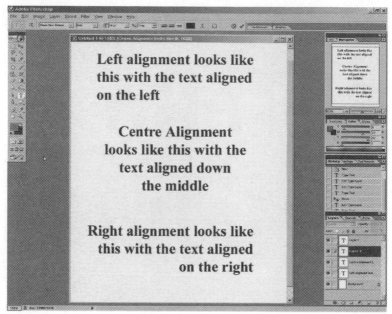

Fig.8.38 The usual types of text alignment are available

near to but not at the left end of the Options bar is an exception, and this toggles the text between the vertical and horizontal modes. Any text on the current layer will change to suit changes in the setting of this button. To the right of this there is the usual font menu that lists all the available fonts (Figure 8.36). There is no preview facility so that you can see what each font looks like, but some text placed on the current layer will change to the selected font. You can quickly try out a few likely fonts.

Moving along the Options bar to the right, the next menu provides text styles such as Regular, Italic, and Bold. The available options will probably vary slightly from one font to another. Next to this is a menu that offers a range of text sizes from 6 to 72 points. Other sizes can be obtained by typing the appropriate point size into the textbox. To change the size or style of existing text, select the type tool and the appropriate layer, and then highlight the text by dragging the cursor through it. Then select the required style and (or) text size.

The next menu offers three types of anti-aliasing or it can be switched off. Anti-aliasing is designed to give text a smoother appearance, and it

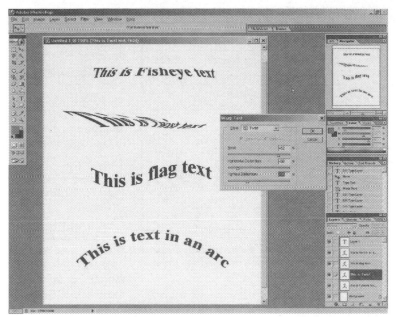

Fig.8.39 A huge range of wrapped text effects are available

operates by using some pixels around the edges of characters at a colour half way between those used for the text and the background. This can be seen in the zoomed view of Figure 8.37 where the text at the top has Strong anti-aliasing and the text at the bottom has none. Apart from a better general appearance, anti-aliasing can make small text more legible. It is particularly good when it is used with fonts that have a tendency to merge adjacent letters. Anti-aliasing is often used when producing web pages, but it is generally less useful when producing printed pages.

Next there are three buttons that provide left, centre, and right alignment (Figure 8.38). Fully aligned (justified) text is not available. To the right of this is the button that is used to set the text colour, and operating this button produces the standard Color Picker. The next button is used to produce wrapped text, and operating it produces a small dialogue box (Figure 8.39). This offers a choice of 15 types of wrapped text from the Style menu, but the range is effectively much larger because there are three slider controls that permit wide variations within each style. Figure 8.39 includes four examples of wrapped text. The usual types of wrapped text are available, including text in various arcs, flag style text, and twisted

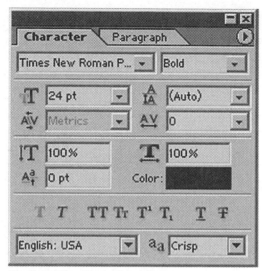

Fig.8.40 The Character palette

text. It is well worth taking some time to experiment with the various options available here. If you need something a bit more artistic than plain text, the wrapped text feature is the place to go.

The final button launches a window that contains the Character and Paragraph palettes (Figures 8.40 and 8.41). Switch between palettes via the tabs at the top of the window. Some of the settings on offer here are the same as those in the options bar, but there are some additional facilities. Starting with the Character palette, beneath the font style menu there are menus for leading and tracking. Leading controls the amount of space between lines of type, so this is irrelevant unless you use a block of text that occupies at least two lines.

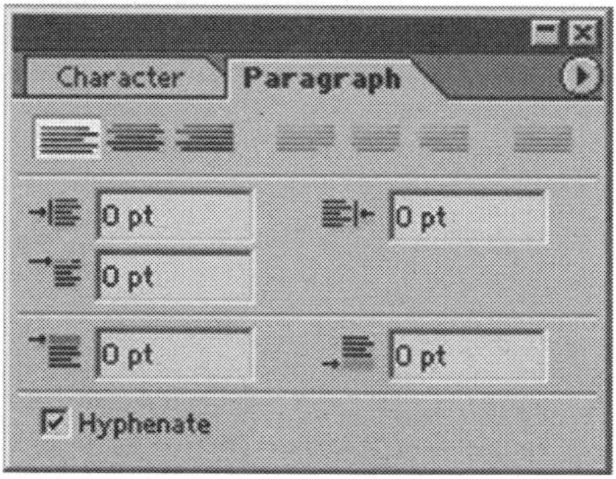

Fig.8.41 The Paragraph palette

Leading is measured from the baseline of one line to the baseline of the next line of text. The value here must be greater than the point size of the characters in order to prevent lines overlapping. The default Auto option can be used if you prefer not to make manual adjustments. This uses a value equal to 120 percent of the text's point size.

Tracking controls the amount of space used between letters in a word. The default value is zero, which gives nicely spaced lettering with most fonts. Use a negative value to bunch the letters together or a positive value to space them further apart. The kerning menu is to the left of the one for tracking. Kerning is related to the spacing between letters in a word, but it goes beyond simply bunching all letters together or moving them all further apart. Kerning provides different spacing depending on which two letters are next to each other, and the text size is also taken into account.

Spacing that looks fine with small lettering often produces what are perceived as huge gaps if the spacing is scaled up with the lettering. Also, letters that have complementary shapes such as A and V appear to be too far apart using normal spacing. Kerning is adjusting the spacing so that it looks right with any combination of letters in any size of type. The default option for kerning is Metrics, which means that Photoshop will use the metrics data built into the font. It is possible to override this by entering a kerning value, but there will usually be no point in doing so.

The textbox beneath the kerning menu controls the vertical scaling. Use a value of more than 100 percent to make the characters taller than normal, or less than 100 percent to produce dumpier letters. The box to the right of this one provides the same function but for the horizontal scaling. Beneath this there is the colour button, and to the left of this is a textbox where a baseline shift value can be entered. This is primarily intended as a means of controlling the shift used for subscript and superscript characters, but it will actually move any selected characters from the baseline by the specified amount.

Moving on down, there is a row of eight buttons that are new in Photoshop 7. From left to right these are:

Faux bold

Faux Italic

All capitals

Small capitals

Superscript

Subscript

Underline

Strikethrough

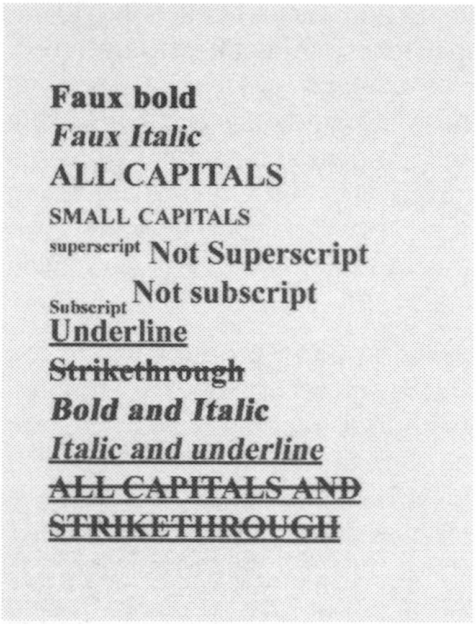

Faux bold
Faux Italic
ALL CAPITALS
SMALL CAPITALS
superscript Not Superscript
Subscript Not subscript
Underline
Strikethrough
Bold and Italic
Italic and underline
ALL CAPITALS AND
STRIKETHROUGH

Fig.8.42　Examples of the text styles

Figure 8.42 shows an example of each style, and it also shows three examples that use a combination of styles.

Beneath the row of eight buttons there is a menu where the correct language can be selected, and another menu that offers the standard anti-aliasing options.

Paragraph palette

In Photoshop terminology, a paragraph is a piece of text that is followed by a carriage return. The Paragraph palette has the three usual alignment buttons in the top left-hand corner. There are additional options to the right of these, including a full justification mode that can be provided by the button at the right end of the line. However, these options are only available when a bounding box is used. If you only need single lines of type there is no point in using a bounding box, but it is advisable to use one for anything more than this. In order to produce a bounding box it is

This is some text that has been entered into a bounding box, and as you will see, text wrapping and even hyphenation are provided when a bounding box is used.

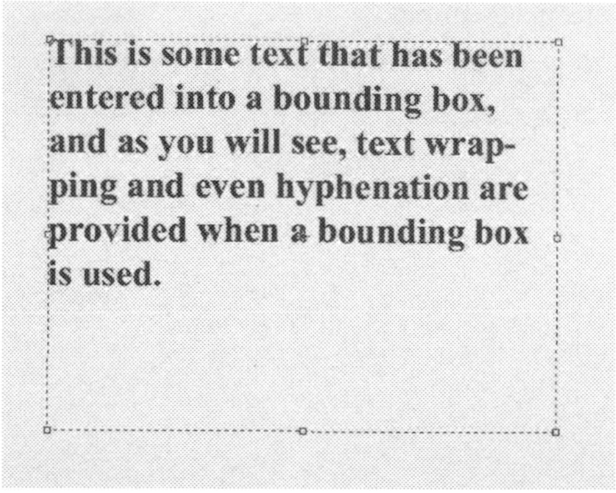

Fig.8.43　Text added to a bounding box

merely necessary to select a Type tool and then drag the box onto the document window.

The Photoshop Type tools then provide something approximating to normal word processing, with the text automatically wrapping around at the ends of lines, and hyphenation added automatically if that option is enabled in the Paragraph palette (Figure 8.43). The bounding box can be resized using the handles, and the text within the box will be automatically reformatted to suit the changes (Figure 8.44). If you try moving the pointer in the vicinity of a corner of the box, in some places it should turn into an arc with an arrowhead at each end. It is then possible to rotate the bounding box by dragging it (Figure 8.45). The origin is normally in the centre of the box, but with the Control key held down it can be dragged to a new position.

This is some text that has been entered
into a bounding box, and as you will
see, text wrapping and even hyphenation are provided when a bounding
box is used.

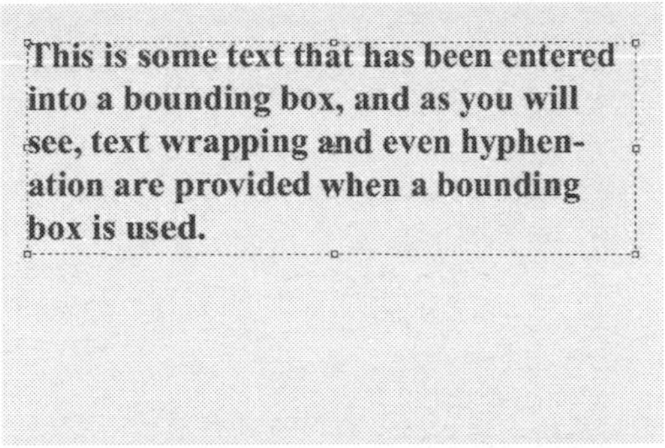

Fig.8.44 The text has automatically reformatted to suit the change in the box

The two text boxes near the top of the paragraph palette enable the text to be indented from the left and right margins. The textbox beneath these enables the first line of each paragraph to be indented. The two textboxes beneath these enable space to be added before and after a paragraph. In other words, the spacing between paragraphs can be made larger than the normal line spacing.

Adding text

As pointed out previously, where anything more than a line of text is required it is usually better to opt for the bounding box method, where more or less the normal word processing facilities are available. If you just need to add the odd line of text, or perhaps two or three

This is some text that has been entered
into a bounding box, and as you will
see, text wrapping and even hyphenation are provided when a bounding
box is used.

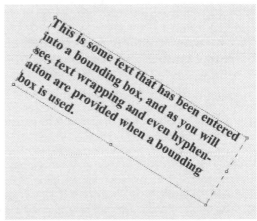

Fig.8.45 The box and text can be rotated

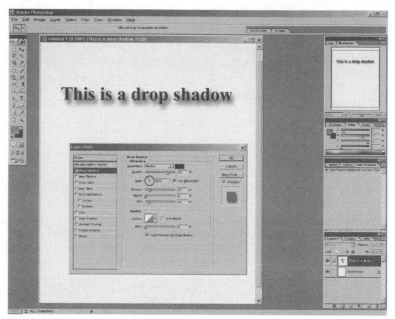

Fig.8.46 There are plenty of options and controls for the drop shadow effect

entirely separate lines of text, then they can be typed direct onto the image. Just select the appropriate Type tool, left-click on the image at the point where you need the text, and start typing. Left aligned will be added to the right of the starting point, right aligned text is added on the left, and centre aligned text is added equally on both sides. The pointer is a vertical line when it is placed over text, indicating that the text can be selected and edited in normal word processor fashion.

Away from the text it changes to the Move pointer, and it is then possible to drag the text to a new position. Where separate lines of text are added it is advisable to place them on individual layers so that they can be positioned independently. Having placed the first line of text, select the Background layer by left-clicking on its entry in the Layers palette. Next, left-click on the image at the point where the next line of text is to be added, and a new text layer will be generated automatically. Add the line of text, selected the Background layer again, and so on until all the text has been entered. Alternatively, just add the new layers manually by selecting New from the Layer menu followed by Layer from the submenu.

Probably most Photoshop users do not need to add substantial amounts of text to images, or do but will add the text after exporting the images to a web page design or desktop publishing program. It is the ability of Photoshop to produce fancy text that is of interest to most users. The wrapped text effects described previously are very useful for this type of thing, and a huge range of effects can be produced. These effects are very

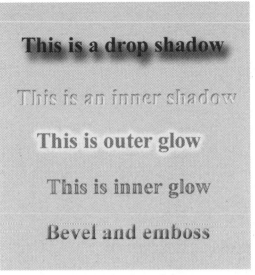

Fig.8.47 *Some of the other effects that are available*

popular for use in web pages, as are drop shadow headlines. Photoshop makes it very easy to add a drop shadow to text.

To try this feature, start by adding some text to a blank page. It Is best to use a fairly large text size so that the drop shadow effect can be seen very clearly. Then go to the Layer menu and select Layer Style followed by Drop Shadow from the submenu that appears. This produces the dialogue box shown in Figure 8.46. There are three slider controls that enable a range of drop shadow effects to be obtained. The Distance slider controls how far the shadow is offset from the text. The Spread control can be adjusted to spread out the shadow, but this also gives a more distinct outline and darkens the shadow. The Size control is really more of a blur control, and enlarging the shadow more than fractionally results in it being totally blurred.

There are other controls available, including the usual Opacity control at the top. This controls the opacity of the shadow and not the text. There is a colour button that produces the standard Color Picker, which can then be used to change the colour of the shadow. By default the shadow is offset downwards and to the right, but the angle can be changed by typing a figure into the appropriate textbox or dragging on the "clock" to

Fig.8.48 The converted text text was skewed and then the Motion Blur filter was used

set the required angle. The control near the bottom of the window permits noise to be introduced into the shadow.

Changes in the settings are immediately applied to the image, so it is easy to experiment with the controls and find the effect you require. In general it is best to use a well blurred shadow if it is near the text. If the shadow is reasonably distinct it produces a double image effect that most people find unpleasant to look at, and the text becomes difficult to read. This is not a problem if the shadow is set well away from the text. There are other effects available from the Layer Styles submenu, and it is a good idea to try experimenting with them. Figure 8.47 shows some of those that are available, but many of the effects only work well in colour. Quite good metallic effects can be obtained using the Bevel and Emboss option together with suitable colours.

Normal selection methods do not work with text, so it is not possible to put a marquee around some text and then use the Transform and Free Transform options in the Edit menu. However, the text can be selected by dragging the text cursor through it, and the Transform and Free Transform options then become available. The usual box with handles

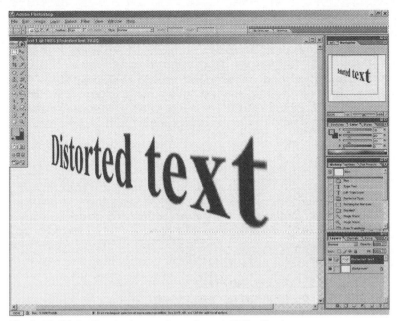

Fig.8.49 Distorting text can give a form of 3D effect

appears around the text when one of these options is selected. Unfortunately, there are some restrictions on the Free Transform facility when it is used with text, and some of the options in the Transform are also unavailable. Text can be skewed and rotated but not distorted for example. It is still useful to manipulate text in this way.

Rasterizing

As pointed out previously, in order to use the full range of Photoshop's clever tricks with text it is necessary to rasterize it. This converts it from text into an image comprised of pixels. The full range of filters, etc., can then be applied, but the text editing facilities are lost. This makes it important to remove any errors from the text before it is rasterized. It is rasterized by making the text's layer the current one and then selecting Rasterize from the Layer menu, and Type from the submenu that appears. Alternatively, if you try to filtering or another facility that requires the text to be rasterized, you will be asked if you wish to rasterize the text so that the processing can be applied. Operate the yes button and the text will be rasterized prior to the filtering or other effect being applied.

Once the text has been converted it can be selected using the normal methods and the whole range of processes becomes available. In Figure 8.48 some text has been added to the photograph of the tortoise. After conversion it was skewed and a small amount of Motion Blur filtering was applied. In Figure 8.49 the text has been selected and the distorted to give a sort of 3D effect, with the text seeming to recede into the distance.

Finally

It is not possible to cover every facet of Photoshop in a book this size, but using the methods described herein it is possible to get the optimum technical quality from any image, add text and creative effects, and cover up blemishes or unwanted objects in images. In the end there is only one way to get the most from a program such as Photoshop, and that is to spend time using it, explore various possibilities, and use your imagination.

Points to remember

Photoshop has a huge range of built-in filters, and many more are available as so called plug-ins. Filters can be used to produce weird effects, blur backgrounds, sharpen slightly blurred images, or add artistic effects.

The Extract filter is similar to a selection method, but strictly speaking it does not produce a selection. It filters the parts of an image that you wish to retain from those that you wish to discard.

If a photograph has a distracting background, selecting and severely blurring it usually cures the problem. Blurring everything except the main subject can help to focus attention on the main subject.

A soft focus effect is produced by mixing a sharp image with one that has been massively blurred. Adding a lot of Gaussian blur and then fading the filtering is the easiest way of producing a soft focus effect using Photoshop.

Smart Blur filtering is useful for removing unwanted textures while leaving edges sharp. It is a very useful tool for producing flattering portraits that make the sitter look many years younger.

Various sharpening filters are available when using Photoshop. These filters all operate in basically the same way, which is to provide localised increases in contrast. They are only effective with pictures that are slightly "soft". The Sharpen edges filter is useful for sharpening edges while leaving everything else untouched. The Unsharp Mask filter gives tremendous control over the filtering, and is the choice of professionals.

Small amounts of text can be typed direct onto the image. With larger amounts it is generally better to put the text into a bounding box. Something approximating to normal word processing facilities are then available.

Numerous special effects are available when using text, including drop shadows, 3D effects, and text wrapping. Text can be entered in the form of masks which can then be filled with patterns, painted, and used much like any other masks.

Text must be rasterized before filtering and some other effects can be applied. Rasterizing simply means converting it into a normal image comprised of pixels. It is not possible to use the normal text editing facilities once the conversion has been made, so try to get the text correct before rasterizing it.

Index

Index